HOME
for the SOUL

HOME
for the SOUL

**SUSTAINABLE AND THOUGHTFUL
DECORATING AND DESIGN**

SARA BIRD &
DAN DUCHARS of
The CONTENTed Nest

RYLAND PETERS & SMALL
LONDON • NEW YORK

Senior designer Toni Kay
Senior commissioning editor
  Annabel Morgan
Location research Jess Walton
Head of production
  Patricia Harrington
Art director Leslie Harrington
Editorial director Julia Charles
Publisher Cindy Richards

First published in 2020 by
Ryland Peters & Small
20–21 Jockey's Fields,
London WC1R 4BW
and
341 East 116th Street
New York, NY 10029

www.rylandpeters.com

MIX
Paper from
responsible sources
FSC® C106563
FSC
www.fsc.org

Text copyright © The CONTENTed
Nest 2020
Design and photographs copyright
© Ryland Peters & Small 2020
10 9 8 7 6

ISBN 978-1-78879-241-7

A CIP record for this book is
available from the British Library.

Library of Congress CIP data has
been applied for.

Printed and bound in China

CONTENTS

INTRODUCTION

Our homes. They invite and welcome, are a space for us to share and enjoy, for making memories. They offer us a backdrop to personalize and are places we call our own. But in today's fast-paced world, where haste and waste often dominate, we seem to be at a tipping point when it comes to how we design, decorate and inhabit our own spaces.

Thankfully, a shift in awareness means we are more mindful about our ecological footprints and how we use the planet's resources. There's a general move towards reducing waste and consumption. Many of us are adopting a slower, more gradual approach to everyday living. And we are realizing that constantly acquiring new stuff and chasing trends doesn't necessarily make for a nurturing, health-giving, happy home.

We wanted to create this book to discover how our homes could be more sustainable and less harmful both to the environment and to us. There are suggestions for choosing all the elements that make up a home, from paint to furniture to display ideas, as well as ideas for simple but appealing craft projects

that add quirky decorative touches. We also visit some carefully chosen homes, both large and small, new and old. They are all different but have one thing in common – these are personal spaces that offer a glimpse of their owners' souls.

We hope the book will inspire you to take a fresh look at your own surroundings. No matter how new or old your home, whether it's owned or rented, shared or you live alone, it should speak of your sense of style, your story, your passions and interests. If it does this and manages not to tread too heavily on our planet, then you have truly created a home for your soul.

1

THE ELEMENTS

PAINT & PALETTES

From the four walls of each room to smaller decorative details and architectural features, our homes provide us with countless opportunities to use paint and colour to add character and atmosphere.

Glossy and fresh or time-worn and weathered, paint has enormous versatility in terms of both appearance and colour. It can be applied to all manner of surfaces and objects for an immediate update, speedily transforming the appearance or mood of a room, a piece of furniture or even just a decorative accessory with only a couple of coats.

Choosing a suitable colour can be more challenging. The right palette can unify difficult spaces and make an interior appear bigger or small than it really is. Colour lends itself to all sorts of visual tricks. Many of the soulful homes in this book boast pale, neutral schemes that provide a backdrop to busy living areas, assorted possessions and decorative details. Others have a dark, moody decor that provides a tranquil, contemplative vibe. Your palette will be a personal decision, but there is ample inspiration here.

Paint is the medium of choice when it comes to upcycling, as it allows us to turn something neglected or unloved into a desirable object. Pieces of furniture found by the side of the road or in charity shops/thrift stores can be given a new lease of life for the price of a can of paint plus a little bit of prep. The results are treasured pieces that have been saved from landfill – a satisfying result.

Thankfully eco-friendly paint is now a huge industry. Solvent-free, organic and vegan paints are available and there are even options that can purify the air in our homes. And not only are these paints less harmful, but they have ethical credentials too.

SOFT AND SUBTLE
For a peaceful feel, try blending pale shades for mood-enhancing interiors. Gentle greys, subdued blues and dusty pinks all contribute to a sophisticated pastel scheme (this page and opposite). Colour is not the only way to add interest – distressed paint finishes will bring texture to a scheme. Vintage items often have flaking paintwork (top right) and this look can be mimicked by a rubbed-back paint finish (right).

COMPLEMENT AND CONTRAST

Dark and moody shades and monochrome schemes are part of a continuing trend that's only growing in popularity. Rich, dark palettes work across many styles, from classic to ethnic, and provide an effective backdrop for furniture and decorative details. Far from stark, dark walls can offer a smart, tailored effect or a homely, cosy vibe (opposite). Monochrome schemes are simple and effective, whether they rely on the contrast between black and white or simply adhere to one colour choice. In this kitchen, salvaged louvre shutters retain their original paintwork, which brings interesting texture to the room (above). Meanwhile, a tranquil all-white bathroom is prevented from feeling clinical thanks to its well-worn painted floorboards and the warm tones of the wood showing through (left).

ALL IN THE DETAILS

Paint has transformative qualities. It can demarcate different zones in an open-plan space, as with this staircase (above right). In a home that's lacking in architectural details, paint effects will add interest to white walls (top left), while a board covered in chalkboard paint allows for spontaneous creativity (opposite). Decorative details add depth – paint the back of a unit (above left) or the inside of a glazed cabinet (top right). All for the price of a pot of paint!

LAYERED AND LIVED IN

Weathered, well-worn and scuffed finishes are a charming way to bring shabby-chic style and tactile touches to a home. Try lightly sanding down painted wood or mixing sand into your chosen paint for a textured finish. Chalk paint will also bring a subtle matt effect and can be used on furniture and decorative accessories, a technique that has been used cleverly on the large urn (left).

CREATE YOUR OWN

Paint is a simple, easily available and inexpensive means of decorating and there are many techniques and ideas to try. It's a great way of adding colour to a home or introducing a change of pace or other visual interest. Paint is also the perfect way to reinvent something old and tired or to personalize an object. Best of all, it doesn't cost the earth, especially if you use up leftovers and ask family if they have any to pass on. Crafting is also a good way to use up sample pots bought for colour testing. Have fun with paint and experiment with creative methods such as stamping, stencilling, colour-blocking and dipping.

WALL ART

Lift spirits in an instant with an eyecatching splash of seasonal shades. For a stylish colour-block effect, roll out a large piece of paper or white cotton or a ready-prepared canvas and tape off a central zone with masking tape. Now simply dab on your preferred paint (sample pot leftovers are ideal). Remove the tape while the paint is still a bit damp, then once it's dry clip the paper to a rod or ruler and hang up with twine. Layering complementary colours adds variety and character.

PAINTED BASKETS

Add character to plain baskets by adding a bold band of contrasting colour. Apply masking tape to the surface of the basket to ensure neat edges, then sponge on your chosen shade with a foam-based brush for an even application that allows the texture of the weave to show through. Chalk paints are particularly good for this technique. Allow the paint to dry, then you're all set to use your basket for storage or shopping.

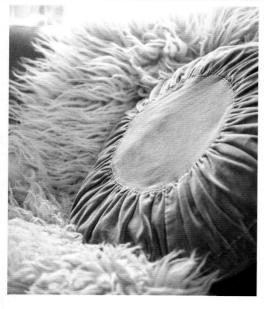

FABRIC & TEXTILES

When it comes to picking fabric, in a soulful home the obvious choice will be natural fibres such as cotton, linen and wool. Also consider vintage options. All will bring comfort and add texture and warmth to a home.

Both decorative and functional, fabrics and other textiles are used on upholstery, to screen windows, to soften the floors beneath our feet and to dress our beds and keep us warm while we sleep. Snug or airy, robust or delicate, they soften hard edges, add elegance to simple settings, cover up less attractive pieces of furniture and bring personality to a home. They are also a perfect hand-me-down. Vintage textiles such as patchwork quilts and Welsh blankets can be repurposed or even fashioned into a new piece that holds fond memories and can be passed down through the generations.

Although synthetic fabrics have their uses, natural fibres are superior in appearance and texture. Look for Oeko-Tex certified textiles, which have been tested and certified to be free of harmful chemicals. Organic cotton is a good choice as it's grown without pesticides or fertilizers – check for Organic Content Standard or GOTS (Global Organic Textile Standard) labels. Hemp is a highly sustainable fibre as is linen, derived from the flax plant. Natural man-made fabrics include lyocell, which is manufactured from wood pulp and makes extremely soft bedding.

Fabrics and textiles are endlessly versatile – choose between luxurious velvet, quilted voile bedspreads, flatweave rugs and cool cotton sheeting, to name but a few. They can be dyed, printed, embroidered and embellished then pleated and pressed to make anything from a simple linen dishcloth to floor-length curtains. Our homes would not be the same without these textures to snuggle, stroke, drape or shelter beneath.

SOFT AND GENTLE
Fabric offers many different tones and textures. Undyed linen allows the sunlight to filter through, transforming it into something almost magical (centre left). It also drapes beautifully, lending itself to graceful curtains (opposite). Velvet has a dense pile that begs to be stroked and makes for wonderfully inviting cushions (above and below left). Interesting features such as pleats and tucks all add to the pleasing visual spectacle.

RECYCLING THE MEMORIES

There is a certain charm to vintage textiles. Sometimes this is down to the way they have been made and finished, especially if they are handmade. They may have developed a patina from years of use. Or perhaps we love them because they have been passed down the generations. Don't be afraid to rethink their purpose, using a bedpread to cover a sofa (above) or tray cloth as a curtain, for example (far right). Alternatively, vintage textures can be upcycled. Try embroidering an old fabric lampshade (right) or appliquéing lace doilies to a simple white blind (opposite).

SCREEN AND SEW

Clipped up, draped or tied in place, a simple length of fabric can be used to create an instant screen to provide privacy, block sunlight or both (opposite). While more formal curtains have their place, a sheet doubled over a pole can work just as well. Winter months call for cosy textures such as pleated velvet, nubbly bouclé, hand knits and even faux fur (this page). Table linens in subdued pastel shades are perfect when spring arrives (above left).

ADD PATTERN AND COLOUR

Cushions are a brilliant way to add a flash of colour or a pattern pop to lift a cosy corner, as seen on this daybed. They are an inexpensive way to be bold and add character, even humour, to your home. As your confidence grows, introduce more pattern or colour for an individual look.

CREATE YOUR OWN

Making something with fabric can seem a little intimidating to a non-sewer, but there are plenty of no-sew options. Fabric can be wrapped, draped, clipped and stapled into place. There are also crafts that rely on tying techniques, such as ragging and plaiting, where only a pair of scissors is required. Heat-bonded tape enables fabrics to be fixed together when hemming curtains, for example. Stitching simple square cushions is a good place for beginners to start, and for confident sewers, the options are endless – patchwork, appliqué, needlepoint, embroidery and quilting are just a few.

DOILY-STENCILLED CUSHIONS

This is a lovely way to update old linens and cushions using paper doilies as a ready-made stencil. With the fabric laid flat on a table, tape the doily to the material on one side. Using a dryish brush, dab eco-friendly fabric paint onto the doily. The secret is not to overload the brush, as then you will lose the intricacies of the doily design. Allow to dry thoroughly before ironing the reverse of the fabric to fix the paint.

BUTTONED NAPKINS

Update plain table napkins with attractive vintage or repurposed buttons snipped from clothing. If you don't have plain napkins, look on ebay for matching sets. Simply press the napkins, then attach the buttons to one corner with a couple of firm stitches so they are secured in place. There's no need for precision – a randomly scattered look is the aim here.

TEXTURE

The sense of touch is important for our wellbeing and the surfaces that surround us should offer tactile and sensory benefits. Texture also contributes to the look of our homes, adding visual interest, contrast and personality.

Not many of us have the chance to choose the building materials for our home unless it's a new build, but we are able to transform what's already in place by papering, panelling or otherwise covering existing surfaces. Almost anything can be used on all manner of areas. Old wooden floorboards can be reinvented as cladding or shelving or built-in storage, metal sheeting can wrap round kitchen worksurfaces, walls can be covered in fabric, mirrored or glass panels as well as wallpaper or woven natural fibres. Durable textures such as wood and metal can be reused and reimagined. If covering an existing surface is not the right solution, then we can expose, rub down and chip away at layers of paint, plaster or paper to reveal the true nature of what lies beneath.

There are many natural and eco-friendly textures and techniques available. Limewash paint is sustainable and allows a building to breathe, and there are also natural lime plastering techniques such as Tadelakt. Other possibilities include bamboo and cork wall coverings, both of which offer excellent insulation. There's even concrete made from hemp and recycled materials.

If you're not in a position to make changes to your surfaces, it's also possible to add texture in the form of fabrics and textiles, furniture and decorative accessories. Look for intriguing surfaces such as time-worn wood, pitted metal and age-spotted mirrors. These will provide contrast and bring character – a good solution for anyone in rental accommodation who cannot change their decor.

MATT AND GLOSS
When it comes to texture, there is beauty in the imperfect with irregular features lending natural appeal. Chalk paint highlights a wall's dimples and depressions, adding depth and interest (opposite). Small details can contribute contrasting texture to a scheme. Polished granite magnifies a vase's pebbled finish, the sheen of leather picks up the gleam of polished wood and a metal pot stands out against a velvety wall (this page).

ROUGH AND SMOOTH

Rough cut and hewn, or planed, sanded and oiled, humble wood brings beauty and vitality to every interior. Here, both recycled and FSC®-certified wood has been used to cover walls, floors and even ceilings, creating a cosy cabin vibe (opposite). In a more minimalist home, just a few bare branches are enough to bring the comforting, tactile presence of natural wood into the interior (this page).

COATING AND CONTOURING

Cladding and covering brings character with each and every layer. It is also an inspiring way to transform banal objects, hand-me-downs, unpretty plastics or dull surfaces. Sometimes a textural spruce up makes a surface instantly intriguing, as with this antique wicker container that was once coated with clay (top left). The decorative balls seen here were originally Christmas decorations, but can be appreciated all year round since they were resurfaced (centre right). Tadelakt plaster has been applied near a basin – not only does it look stylish, it's also waterproof (bottom left). Surfaces can be rubbed back and distressed to offer intriguing effects, as with these shutters (top right) and a mirror that was accidently aged from being left outside and now gently reflects features in its foxed glass (centre left). Paint effects can be used to add an appealing finish that mimics the mottled look of bare plaster (bottom right). Painterly silhouettes ripple over a chalk-painted wall (opposite).

CREATE YOUR OWN

When it comes to crafting, there are many easy methods to add texture. For instant patina, try gently sanding down painted wooden pieces so the warm tones and grain of the wood show through. Textured or handmade paper can be pasted onto a section of wall or used to cover smaller items such as storage boxes and books. Update plain lampshades or pendants with sheets of ready woven cane. And don't worry about less than perfect finishes. Dents, scuffs, chips and scrapes add character to a home.

CLAY-COVERED KITCHENALIA

Leftover plastic plates and flatware can be given a new lease of life with a coating of air-dry modelling clay. Make sure your chosen items are clean and dry then cover the surface with the clay, pressing it into place. Either leave the surface smooth or stamp in interesting impressions then leave it to dry. If desired, you can give your items a layer of clay paint to enhance the texture.

PAPER-COVERED BOOKS

Reuse packaging by covering books and notebooks in brown paper. Cut and flatten out the bag to its largest extent, then place the book on top open and face up. Fold excess paper over the top and sides of the book, carefully snipping where the spine lies in line with the top and the bottom of the book. Secure the paper in place with tape – brown paper tape is ideal – and tuck the narrow spine section down the inside of the lining.

TEXTURE ADDS INTEREST

Reclaimed painted wooden planks add texture to two alcoves fitted with shelves (opposite). The chipped paint of the old planks provides textural contrast with the smooth white walls and painted cupboards and the wood showing through tones perfectly with the weathered pine floorboards.

FURNITURE, STORAGE & LIGHTING

The essential building blocks of the home, our furniture, fixtures and fittings are key to the way we live. Get these elements right, and your home will work harder, run more smoothly and look better too.

Items of furniture, storage and lighting have a practical role to play in our homes. They provide solutions to everyday problems – dark corners and cluttered spaces – and meet specific needs – a place for homework, somewhere to curl up with a book.

Pieces of furniture are often large and expensive, so it's important to get them right. Most people prefer to buy items such as sofas and beds new rather than second-hand, and if this is the case look for the best quality you can afford as well as eco-friendly manufacturing processes, ethical values and certifications from organizations such as the FSC® to give peace of mind. However, new furniture will always carry a higher carbon footprint than older pieces. Antique and vintage items are often more robust, too, as they were built to last from better-quality materials. They also add personality to a home in the way a flat-pack table never can.

When it comes to storage, for maximum flexibility aim for a blend of fitted/built-in and freestanding. Look for vintage pieces such as dresser/hutches, chests, trunks and lockers. As well as playing a practical role, such items are also decorative and chips, scuffs and a well-worn patina only adds to their appeal.

Aim to have at least four different lighting sources in each room, from pendants and wall fittings to table lamps and desk lights. These can be a good way to introduce more texture, pattern, colour and decorative interest. Don't forget candlelight – the most soulful light of all.

PUT IT AWAY

Storage is essential for a calm and composed home. Vintage cabinets, closets and armoires and other freestanding storage will accommodate all manner of items and allow interiors to function well with space to breathe (this page and opposite). Choose vintage items to bring soul and personality to an interior. Long-lived pieces such as this leather armchair make a home feel established and timeless (right).

GLEAM AND SPARKLE

A fantastic source of originality, lamps in their many manifestations bring style as well as illumination to our interiors. While task lighting tends to be more functional, you can express your sense of style with dramatic pendants and unusual statement lighting in retro, modern and vintage styles. Gleaming and pierced metal, sparkling beaded fittings and woven designs, as shown on these pages, all produce attractive effects as they filter artificial light. If you are buying vintage lighting, make sure the fitting is rewired to the appropriate modern specifications.

TEMPER TECHNOLOGY

Devices, electronics and gadgets are part of modern life but it's good to have a break from them. This is easier if screens are stored in cupboards or behind doors. This television has been concealed behind beautiful bespoke doors constructed from a set of vintage floral prints. Putting such items out of sight allows us gizmo-free down time to concentrate on other things.

PAST AND PRESENT

Gone are the days of buying a matchy-matchy three-piece suite. It's far more interesting to gradually source furniture as and when the need arises (this page). Embrace the slow-living approach and you will find that existing pieces will easily absorb newcomers. When you're shopping, look out for well-made antique or vintage items or modern design classics and buy for the long term, knowing the pieces will be well used and well loved. To ring the changes in an interior, swap in decorative accessories, plants and flowers to signal changing themes and seasons.

CREATE YOUR OWN

Mending or revitalizing discarded or damaged pieces of furniture, storage or lighting takes time and ingenuity. Repairing or repainting might be the obvious fix, but there are other crafty hacks. Try swapping the legs on a chest or sofa, adding pretty new handles or using old drawers to construct storage or shelving units. Cover tired lampshades in fabric or yarn. If something is broken beyond repair, before you throw it away make sure to salvage old knobs, drawer pulls, latches or handles. All can be reused in new craft projects – most satisfying.

WOVEN-BACKED CHAIR

Damaged furniture can live to see another day with a smart rethink. Take this chair, which now features a new back made from upholstery tape and ribbon. Wind lengths of the tape from side to side of the chair back to provide a horizontal framework. Now take the ribbon and, going from top to bottom, weave it in and out of the tape at regular intervals until you have created a woven framework. Tie knots at the back for comfort and to give a neater finish.

DRAWER STORAGE

If a piece of furniture really has had its day, the drawers might still have a use. They can easily be stacked or arranged to create a shelving unit like this one on a desktop. Such storage has the benefit that it can be immediately repositioned or reconfigured as your storage requirements change.

DINING CHAIRS

Recovering the seats on chairs gives them an immediate facelift and is surprisingly simple, even if you're not that crafty. As well as sufficient fabric for the number of chairs, you will need a staple gun. Wrap the fabric over each seat pad then staple in place. It's a great way of uniting mismatched seating (opposite).

Dare
to be
ro...

Jo Behari & Alison Winfield-Chislett

...yle   Amanda Brooks

MINDFULNESS

THE DEADLY DICTIONARIES   SLOTH

ON DISPLAY

Revealing character, tastes, interests and even humour, our treasured belongings and accessories stimulate us, connect us to the seasons, make us smile and provide an insight as to who we are and how we live.

Hung on a wall, propped on a shelf, arranged on a bookcase – having our favourite items displayed around us is a way of sharing our passions. The things we choose to surround ourselves with give others a fascinating insight into our hobbies, travels, history and so much more. Everything from an inherited collection of antique glass to a handful of family photographs can make for a great display that will enliven an interior and spark happy memories every day.

Decorative items and treasures bring soul to a home – they have the ability to personalize a room, liven up a dark corner and add interesting silhouettes. It's best when these items are slowly acquired over time – putting old and new pieces together make a home look more authentic.

Displays don't just look good. They can also be a pleasure to devise and assemble, and the way things are arranged often reveal our character traits – lined up and orderly or artfully casual and off-the-cuff? Maximalist arrangements for maximum impact, or calm and restrained vignettes?

Collections don't have to be items of great value – you can showcase everyday items too. Most things look good en masse, whether it's hand-thrown mugs, baskets, vases or straw hats – the list is endless. Showcasing ordinary items can elevate them into something intriguing. In the kitchen, open shelves offer an opportunity to display tableware, glasses and other items in regular use, such as food that's attractively packaged or dried goods decanted into glass jars.

A PLACE FOR EVERYTHING

All manner of surfaces and shelving can be used for a display. Here shelves have been hung close to a bed so bedtime reading and a glass of water are close to hand (opposite). If you can't hang shelves, try hooks and hang regularly used items within easy reach (above right) or use a piece of furniture for a thoughtful arrangement (right). A shelf by a window is the perfect place for plants to gather (above centre).

SMART CASUAL

We all have kitchen- and tableware and it can make for a charming display. Open shelves and small units are an excellent place to stack all those plates and glasses used regularly so they don't gather dust and are within easy reach when cooking and serving food (above and below right). A glazed cabinet like this vintage example is a handsome way to safely display delicate and fragile glassware that isn't in everyday use (opposite).

WALL TO WALL

A gallery of happy memories is a great idea for bare walls and staircases are particularly useful with their large expanses (above). It's a good idea to plan where pictures might hang, although a more fluid approach is fine if there are going to be regular additions and updates. If you only have a small patch of wall available, use that for a more informal pinboard effect, with images that can be put up or taken down in an instant (right).

CHARACTER AND HUMOUR

Have fun arranging and displaying purely decorative pieces – vintage finds, clothes, souvenirs and humorous pieces. A mannequin is adorned with clothes and jewellery that evoke happy memories (above left). A quirky china cactus adds a pop of colour to a dark corner (above right). A row of elegant figurines catch the light on a narrow windowsill (below right) while a terracotta bust brings a stately quality to a humble wooden chest (below left).

STATEMENT STYLE

Display is a powerful tool that can set the tone for different spaces in the home. We might want more casual arrangements in everyday or family areas, but some rooms are suited to something more formal. This hallway is a masterclass in using unexpected and oversized accessories for a handsome touch on entering.

CREATE YOUR OWN

The way we display and arrange our treasures is as important as the treasures themselves. Empty walls beg to be filled with artworks or framed family photos. Furniture and other surfaces offer the opportunity for carefully curated decorative vignettes. Often a display is more effective if the items are linked in some way – by colour, use or theme. Keep displays accessible so you can swap things round or ring the changes with the passing seasons. And if you're something of a collector, you'll want to build in space for your collection to grow.

CHICKEN WIRE NOTICEBOARD

An old mirror or picture frame can easily take on a new use even if the back has been lost or damaged. Remove any remaining bits of casing then measure the frame and cut a length of chicken wire that will just fit over the aperture. Lay the frame face down then stretch and staple-gun the wire into place. Dress your noticeboard with notes, cards and ideas kept in place with mini clips, clothes pegs or magnets.

MEMORY JAR

Simple glass food jars can make a lovely and unusual alternative to the classic photo frame for favourite pictures. Wash out and dry the jars so they are sparkling. Now choose images to fit and simply place them inside. Foliage, flowers and other interesting finds such as shells or feathers can be added to spark additional memories.

STOW IT AWAY

Open pigeonholes offer abundant and versatile storage as each cubbyhole can be filled with all manner of items, both decorative and practical (opposite). Here, books jostle with magazines and work paraphernalia sits alongside family photographs but all in a structured and contained manner.

A SENSE OF WELLBEING

Creating a truly nurturing home for the soul is key to finding happiness and health. Seek wellbeing by connecting with your home, inspiring all your senses and making eco-friendly lifestyle choices.

Alongside all the practicalities of homemaking, how we feel about being inside our home is just as important. The awareness and sensation of being at home should be comforting and reassuring. Home provides us with a familiar backdrop, allowing us to step back from our busy lives. It's also a place where we can engage with mindful approaches to boost our sense of wellbeing.

We can design our homes to improve our quality of life and sense of wellbeing. There's a whole spectrum of possibilities and choices. Some are easy to implement, like visual pick-me-ups such as mood-boosting colours and living with plants to make us feel better. Other improvements require bigger

changes, such as using eco-friendly paints with lower VOCs (volatile organic compounds), investing in plug-in air purifiers and installing water filters. Then there are simple lifestyle changes that enhance wellbeing, such as opening the windows, getting plenty of sleep and choosing items that appeal to our senses of touch, taste and smell.

Putting a creative spin on things presents us with another source of contentment. Reinventing items that we find or inherit and making the most of what we have makes us feel good, as does choosing ethically produced goods, supporting artisan makers and seeking ways to cut down on waste and curb our own environmental footprint.

KEEP IT CLEAN
For wellbeing, source eco-friendly non-toxic paint and dry any that's left over in an ice-cube tray to absorb airborne pollutants (top right). Candles can damage air quality but misting diffusers won't spread pollution in the same way (centre right). Increase access to good scents with fresh herbs (right). The sound and sight of nature and a connection with the natural world will enhance our sense of wellbeing (opposite).

OUTSIDE IN

Our genetic connection to the outside world, or biophilia, is well documented. For a healthy and happy home environment, introduce plants, organic materials and outdoor views wherever possible to promote a sense of creativity and wellbeing (above and opposite).

TACTILE TREASURES

There is something wonderfully therapeutic about tinkering with odds and ends. Changing and rearranging, creating interesting vignettes. Take a 'no rules' approach and mix up new and old mementoes, plants and foraged finds. Crystals can introduce good vibes and transform the energy in your home (above), while burning tied bundles of dried sage is said to purify a space and invite positive energy into a home (right).

SLOW LIVING SIMPLICITY

Take time out to enjoy and process all those small everyday moments. Just being in our home and slowing down gives us the chance to unwind and reconnect with our spiritual side. Stop and watch the world go by or listen to the humming sounds of home life. Factor in small rituals or make time to dream and dawdle. Light incense or a candle and watch the smoke swirl, burn sage to purify the air or hold a crystal in your hand and become aware of its texture and how it reflects and refracts light. Stroke your pets and give them love and attention (this page). Examine and appreciate the pattern that can be found in every grain and groove of natural decorating materials such as wood (opposite). Germinate seeds and watch plants as they slowly grow towards the sun, and sit still for long enough to follow shadows as they move across the ground (below left and right).

CREATE YOUR OWN

The creative process of crafting instills a sense of wellbeing, not only because of the end result but also because of the journey undertaken to learn or perfect a skill. The physical process of making can be calming too, bringing with it almost a meditative quality. Crafts such as paper folding, painting, beadwork, calligraphy or something simple yet repetitive like crocheting or knitting can be a soothing and cathartic pastime. And, of course, handcrafted pieces are something we can pass down and treasure forever – a lasting reminder of the place and the person who made them.

TINNED SUCCULENTS

Even a touch of greenery brings a little joy and these sweet tin planters make a lovely and unusual gift. Cover the base of a small tin with a layer of gritty, free-draining potting compost that comes about halfway up the side of the tin. Water lightly, then transfer your chosen succulents. You may need more compost to anchor the plants in place. Once done, cover the surface of the compost with a sprinkle of gravel and water lightly.

BOTTLE CANDLESTICKS

Don't throw away gorgeous glass bottles but keep them to make seasonal candle holders. Clean thoroughly and remove any labels (white spirit will get rid of stubborn adhesive), then fill with water. Add a drop of bleach-free cleaner to keep the water clear then gently insert herb stems through the neck of the bottle before pushing a candle in the top. If your candle is too large then carve to fit (use a potato peeler); if it's too small wind some twine around the base to broaden.

LOVE TO GROW

Cultivating flowers and plants brings out our nurturing side and is good for the soul. Growing from seed, transferring seedlings and potting on brings valuable moments of peace. Even routine day-to-day tasks such as feeding and watering are soothing and something to be valued. Choose houseplants based on where they are to be grown, the amount of time you can devote to tending them and their rate of growth.

2

THE HOMES

MAXIMALIST

SUSTAINABLE
sanctuary

Catherine's mindful approach to decorating and display is evident in her inspiring home, where repainted and repurposed pieces, quirky artworks and vintage finds all sit harmoniously alongside snug, soothing shades.

OPPOSITE & RIGHT
Character and personality are delivered in an instant on entering Catherine's home. The hallway features an array of eclectic artworks and interesting textures and foliage, with vintage pieces intermingled with more recent buys. An impressive Old Master-style painting dominates, but the selection of differing frames add layers of interest with their bold profiles, glazed inserts and finishes in rich gilt and black.

Creating a stylish city retreat without causing unnecessary waste was Catherine Ashton's aim when it came to her apartment renovation. Bought as a blank canvas, with the rush of urban life just a stone's throw away, the plan was to transform the interior into a place to escape and unwind using elements that were already to hand. Thanks to her decision to combine striking good looks with sensitive sourcing, Catherine has created an inviting home that strikes the right balance between character and comfort.

The starting point was to restructure the flow of the interior. Sections of wall were removed, one of them replaced with an arched opening between the kitchen and living room, and a bulky boiler cupboard was repositioned. Thanks to these tweaks, the modestly sized apartment has been transformed into an open and inviting space that offers pleasing vistas from room to room.

RIGHT
Originally a wall separated the kitchen and the living room, but Catherine knocked a archway through to connect the two spaces. The rounded lines of an archway are replicated in the kitchen beyond, with an oversized clock on the wall. The fun faux cacti seems to wave to us in friendly fashion.

Glossy black surfaces reflect daylight around the kitchen. Warm sunlight is dappled by foliage, casting atmospheric shadows and creating cosy vibes. The polished granite worktops are also reflective, showcasing Catherine's favourite homewares.

ABOVE RIGHT On the kitchen walls, carefully arranged kitchen accessories are displayed alongside artworks for a pleasing still life. The pale wood of the circular chopping boards leaps out from the dark backdrop, while polished copper utensils glow.

With the apartment, Catherine inherited perfectly adequate kitchen and bathroom fittings but they looked tired and characterless. Rather than ripping everything out and starting from scratch, she considered what she could salvage and repurpose. Catherine's vision for the decorative scheme was to create rooms with a composed, restorative feel, so she opted for a dark, cocooning palette. Walls, floors and ceilings were all given a couple of layers of paint and Catherine's favoured eco-friendly brand had the added benefit of offering better coverage per coat. The leftover paint was used to revamp home accessories such as frames and furniture, adding to the cohesive scheme.

The kitchen is a fine example of how existing fixtures can be repurposed and refreshed. Catherine updated all the surfaces, including the mosaic tiles and wooden floor, with a coat of black paint. Most effective is the way the sober hue interacts with the changing light, the glossy tiles

OPPOSITE
The existing kitchen was given a overhaul thanks to a can of black paint. Catherine used it on every surface, and in doing so managed to turn the room's small size on its head. Using just one colour everywhere makes a space feel more expansive and the daylight flooding through the window bounces off metal appliances and handles, adding to the illusion of a larger space.

and floor complementing the softer sheen of the cabinetry and walls. Leafy plants, portraits, decorative accessories and hand-crafted pieces all add charm and character.

The sitting room is a hive of inspiring elements that creatively come together. Keen to create a lived-in look, Catherine sourced vintage furniture, lighting and textiles that bring a cosy and long-established mood to the room, as well as making newer buys feel more settled. During the redecoration, second-hand shops were a key destination where Catherine scooped up reconditioned cabinets, rewired lighting and vintage textiles, all of which contribute to the apartment's

LEFT
Catherine reveals a masterly talent for blending numerous different textures in her living room. The result is a cosy and comfortable retreat. A velvet sofa, battered leather armchair, chunky woollen throws and a sheepskin beg to be stroked and snuggled into. Catherine's houseplants echo the vegetation outside and soften the strong colours.

homely, gradually gathered effect. Inherited pieces and heirlooms rub shoulders with these junk-shop finds and add interest to the interior. In search of unique finishing touches, Catherine commissioned artisans to custom make certain pieces. Her dining furniture was available in one colourway but she requested her own choice of finish, while a kitchen clock she spotted online was recreated by crafters. Her most treasured item is an oversized vintage mirror framed by her partner. The finish is bespoke, with hand-honed detail.

Combining contrasting textures and cherished belongings, the bedroom is a restful space. Unstructured cottons and linens crumple invitingly alongside luxurious velvet, while colourful curios add a personal touch to shelving made from salvaged boards. Recycled light fittings have been chosen for this room; a revamped reading light features an unusual textured wool shade while the elegant chandelier was a lucky brocante find.

ABOVE

In dark corners where plants might not flourish, faux or dried flowers and plants have been used instead. Even faux greenery can offer a biophilic sense of wellbeing, without needing to be watered.

RIGHT

Catherine likes to blend different elements in her scheme. This eclectic, slightly random approach often looks better the busier it gets. In the living room modern, retro and antique pieces all sit happily together, with the odd note of quirk and humour thrown in.

OPPOSITE

When it comes to displaying artworks, Catherine likes to hang them by theme and her portrait collection is given its very own gallery wall. The pictures are arranged salon-style, bringing character and interest to the room. From the ceiling hangs one of her favourite pieces, a hand-beaded clay chandelier from ethical brand Handmade Story.

LEFT & FAR LEFT
Catherine has an eye for a detail. Witty and unusual finds collected over the years such as this metal marionette (left) are clustered together with quirky houseplants to create colourful and appealing vignettes. Mixing different shades, shapes, scales and finishes means that there is a lot going on, but it all looks so good.

Even the pocket-sized bathroom underwent a mini makeover. The walls were given a coat of lustrous black paint, which proved the perfect foil for the existing white bathroom fixtures. Beside some cost-effective eco-accessories, Catherine's favourite trinkets and houseplants add a sense of individual flair.

This home has been sensitively curated to reveal the homeowner's personality and offers her a place to cherish. The dramatic decor, the blend of hand-me-downs and witty details, and the balance of light and shade make for a beautiful space that soothes, inspires and uplifts.

OPPOSITE
Textural heaven, the bed is dressed with multiple layers of linens to create the most inviting of places to lie. On the wall, a gold mirror reflects the rich jewelled hues of the bedding as well as the glinting prisms of Catherine's treasured chandelier.

RIGHT
In the small bathroom, a large mirror has been installed to maximize the sense of space. It also reflects an elegant crystal chandelier that in itself adds additional sparkle and a sense of luxury to the simple scheme.

COLLECTIVE *spirit*

Comfortable and carefree, Clare Lattin's home abounds with easy-going appeal, combining tranquil corners with sociable spaces in a beautiful warehouse conversion that's peppered with plentiful mementoes and keepsakes.

Clare Lattin's home is both a hive of activity and a cosy and calming place of retreat. Thanks to her busy life as a restaurateur she is on the go all the time so home needs to be a restorative space, bringing instant respite as she closes her front door behind her.

Clare's apartment is situated in a 1920s warehouse conversion, and it was the community spirit in the building that most appealed to her on first viewing. All the apartments open onto a central space,

LEFT & RIGHT
The heart of the home, Clare's kitchen is a casually laid out affair with unfitted units and open shelves. Surfaces are covered with an assortment of boards, pots and crocks that provide functional ornament. In pride of place is Clare's oversized table surrounded by a collection of vintage Thonet chairs, which travelled with her from a former home. Providing plenty of daylight are the handsome warehouse windows. The sill is used as a mini nursery for a collection of houseplants.

so the comings and goings of everyday living are shared. When it came to the decor, Clare wanted to bring the building's sociable, friendly ethos into the apartment rather than getting hung up on any particular design scheme. For her, long dinners with friends, kitchen-sink catch-ups and chats over coffee are more important than the latest interior trends, so her goal was to create a homely, welcoming space within the existing framework.

Early on, some walls were knocked through but Clare was mindful that she wanted to retain a sense of cosiness, as this can so easily be lost in an open-plan warehouse interior. Accordingly, Clare has zoned the space using different textures, floor heights, furniture and screening, and balanced the open-plan free-flow of the interior with quiet corners. Simple linen curtaining provides privacy between spaces, but there are also plentiful seating areas that offer a sociable mood. Despite the zoning, Clare's chosen palette gives the apartment

ABOVE
Souvenirs from exotic travels and hanging planters dress a shelf, adding a global touch to Clare's office space. Baskets are a great way to add texture to a white backdrop. Herbs have been hung up to dry on a small wooden rail.

RIGHT
Bare bricks are a feature of this warehouse conversion and inject a note of warmth and texture. To the side of the kitchen, an office nook has been created with a desk positioned beneath one of the soaring metal-framed windows

OPPOSITE
Clare has used vintage linens to screen the sunlight and to demarcate different areas in her home. Casually hung from rods or hooked over doors, these drapes soften the industrial backdrop. They also offer privacy, covering the large glazed entrance doors.

"A delightful atmosphere prevails here, with Clare's spirit shining through the decorative choices."

a cohesive feel. Nature is her inspiration, and the soft white walls are warmed with earthy browns and ochres enlivened with the odd splash of yellow or green.

The kitchen is the centrepiece of the interior and the backbone of Clare's home. Despite being a functional area, it has a friendly disposition and Clare can often be found here cooking or mingling with friends. Much of her home life revolves around the large vintage dining table, which she has carried with her from home to home. Her collection of antique chairs provide elegant seating, with their punched seat patterns adding detail to the dining space. Practical open shelving is home to stacks of china while oversized

baskets offer ample storage. The walls are hung with the tools of Clare's trade: a joyful jumble of jars, pots and pans.

Just beyond the kitchen, the curtained study area is conducive to planning and reading, while the living area is designed for leisurely lazing. Even these spaces are zoned within their zones. The study space features a cosy daybed that's perfectly positioned for quick work breaks, while the living area has a vintage rocker positioned invitingly in the reading nook.

Clare's decor has evolved over time, and her home is a busy yet harmonious mix of everyday items and unexpected finds. This is a calm, uncluttered space, adorned with an abundance of well-loved pieces, most of

OPPOSITE
A half-wall is a clever way to divide two different spaces while retaining an open-plan feel, as has been done with the kitchen and living room here. The top is finished with reclaimed scaffold planks and is an ideal storage-cum-display space for Clare's many culinary ingredients.

ABOVE An oversized sofa separates off the living area. This space is used for various activities so there are several different seating options, many of them vintage.

RIGHT

Rather than clearing them away, Clare leaves her art and craft equipment ready for when the mood might strike. Bringing colour, texture and visual interest, they also offer an insight into Clare's creative side.

FAR RIGHT

Layered rugs are warm underfoot and create sound and heat insulation as well as adding decorative detailing to a large open space. Despite their different designs, the rugs draw on the same tonal palette. The retro Ercol-style bench offers versatile seating as it's light and easy to move

them old but with a smattering of new items. These sit happily alongside a jungly array of plants and dried flowers.

A delightful atmosphere prevails here, with Clare's spirit shining through the decorative choices. Textiles brought back from her travels, worn vintage furniture, woven baskets and washed linens soften the scuffed floors, painted brick and metal beams. Sunlight spills across steel, glass, mirrors and ceramics. Even the darkest corners of the apartment are exquisitely illuminated, thanks to the installation of a vintage glass door in the bathroom and a bedroom wall that features internal windows that allow light to pass through.

LEFT

Large open shelving units line a corner of the living area's walls. Filled with many of the accessories Clare uses for her hobbies and pastimes, they are a practical and well-used addition to the space. The shelves are charmingly higgledy-piggledy rather than over curated, and bring colour, personality and visual interest to the simple white backdrop.

To draw the eye and introduce
a change of pace the staircase
has been painted a crisp black.
Clare is not one to miss the
opportunity for a creative display,
so the treads and a nearby shelf
boast an ever-changing array
of art, books, vases and plants.

RIGHT
There's a change of gear in the bedroom. Wanting to create a calm sleep space, Clare has styled this room more minimally, with less ornament and display. There is more colour here too, with muted pastel bedding and a storm-cloud grey bedspread.

Clare's home is a jostle of juxtapositions that reflect her own character. Although she says she needs to have some things 'just so', she's also relaxed about how things look and more interested in inhabiting a sociable, welcoming home than sticking to rigid interior design rules. When she makes a purchase, she feels a thread leads her back to the source of the item, the making journey it's been on or the retail road that was taken. Instead of rushing her own journey, Clare has gradually brought her home to life, creating a place of simple beauty nestled within an industrial setting.

LEFT & OPPOSITE
The bathroom is calm, feminine and relaxing with powder pink paint coating the only door in the whole apartment (opposite). The pastel shade is complemented by a vintage lace cloth hung over the etched glass window in the door to provide privacy. In keeping with this elegant look, the custom-built concrete sink features stylish vintage taps.

CHARACTER *case*

Blending colourful artworks, treasured keepsakes and 'slow design' principles, Sam Thompson has brought character, life and soul to her new-build family home.

OPPOSITE & BELOW
Colour and pattern offer a warm welcome in the entrance hall. A bold, blowsy botanical-print wallpaper on the wall behind the stairs looks cutting-edge and offers contrast to the white-painted woodwork/trim. The other walls are a gentle plaster pink. Personal treasures are on display and fresh flowers bring the space to life.

Buying a new-build development property was not the plan for Sam Thompson, but she and her family fell for the large space, light and eco-build principles of their now home. The challenge was to make it their own, instil some personality and fit in all their treasured belongings.

Bought in 2014, the house, although designed as a family home, had a tiny kitchen, hardly any built-in storage and lots of blank white walls. But some generous green credentials had been figured in. A living roof and

ABOVE
Sam created this 'good times' gallery on the upper staircase, where only the family pass by. The many framed photos and treasured mementoes are all roughly the same size and shape, allowing recent additions to be swapped in and out as new adventures happen.

BELOW

Sam carved out a space for a pantry as a solution for the lack of storage. The old kitchen units were reinstalled here and her builder covered and sealed the old worktop with a new skimmed finish. Bauwerk Lime Paint was used to cover the walls and add texture. Sam designed wall shelving for food and other provisions, and cubby holes below the worktop hold wine and baskets for linens. A wall rail holds colourful recycling shoppers and bags.

RIGHT & OPPOSITE

The kitchen is a fresh and pretty blend of modern minimal design and quirky upbeat accessories. Thanks to the large island, shelving and deep windowsills, there are settings aplenty for interesting details that temper the boxy shapes of units and appliances. Pretty pastels, elegant lighting, warm materials and pottery and plants add charm here. Sam has mixed high street and designer wares with chainstore finds alongside unique hand-made pieces.

ample insulation have been installed, offering seasonally sympathetic internal temperatures, while daylight is drawn in through the many windows and a large rooflight.

Considering how best to both link and divide the open-plan kitchen-cum-living room and the private spaces opening off the hall and landing space, Sam decided to zone each area. The predominantly white walls provide a clean and cohesive backdrop yet each room has a distinct feature – a colour, pattern or a collection – that gives it an individual voice. Eco-friendly paints and sustainably designed papers and other finishes feature throughout.

A gentle plaster pink shade welcomes visitors as they step through the front door, while a dramatic dark floral wallpaper offers

a change of pace and draws the eye up the staircase. Judicious touches of black are a recurring theme here, bringing a robust edge to the pretty pastel shades of Sam's homewares and accessories.

Shared family time influenced the design of the open-plan living space. Sam is a keen cook with a young family, so she planned a large kitchen that connects to the dining and living areas where the family gather together. In the kitchen, Sam had some of the wall cabinets removed and reclaimed wooden shelving installed in their place. The wood provides a tactile and warming counterpoint to the sleek white units. This simple, modern space has practical surfaces and ample storage, while Sam's kitchenalia, cookware and plants add colour and personality in abundance.

The vibrant kitchen styling extends to the living and dining areas. Sam's love of plants and the wellbeing they bring is evident in the many different varieties flourishing here. There's also much delightful and charismatic artwork, all acquired to mark important family moments, anniversaries and celebrations. Pictures are an important decorative feature but also shape different areas. A favourite space is the staircase gallery of family photographs, prints and images of places the family have visited.

LEFT
Picking exactly the right artworks to display in a room is something of an art form in itself. But you can be sure of one thing: get a wall hang right, and it will offer a window into another world. Sam's pictures were chosen to celebrate birthdays and anniversaries and their vibrant colours and patterns brings personality to this busy family space.

ABOVE & OPPOSITE

Sam has successfully made a large, potentially bland space feel homely by being bold with larger-than-life styling solutions. Her oversized modular sofa is piled high with cushions. The chunky wooden coffee table brings warmth and texture, while mismatched chairs provide seating for all comers. The tiled floor is covered with a Beni Ourain-style rug and colourful paintings hang on the walls, one in an elaborate frame. An eccentric lamp offers humour with its kitsch flamingo base and the finishing touch is a sprinkling of jungle-like plants.

There are a multitude of textural details throughout, and it's safe to say Sam has a real talent for using textiles. Chunky weaves, velvets, tassels and patterned voiles soften the rooms and offer tactile elements. The hard edges of modern technology have been disguised here. The main living area houses the family television, but when not in use it is hidden in a bespoke handmade cabinet so its presence does not dominate family life.

Although she likes to take note of new interiors trends, Sam says that sustainability and slow interiors are a higher priority. Not all her possessions suit her present style, but if they are still in use and fit for purpose, she feels that throwing them away would be wasteful. Many of her belongings have been picked up over the years and followed her from home to home. Rather than discarding an item if it doesn't look quite right, Sam tries hard to make it work

and says a change of position can often work as well as a complete revamp. The well-used sofa will stay for the time being, while Sam's old kitchen table has recently been passed on to her sister. The purchase of any new item is always well considered, with Sam opting to spend her money with companies who care for how things are created and the materials that are used and their impact on the environment.

For Sam, her home is a huge source of happiness, not just because of the way it looks but also because she has so enjoyed the process of its creation. She takes her time to design and decorate and only one project is tackled every year in order to allow for adequate planning. There's no rush here when it comes to creating exactly the right look – Sam is in it for the long haul. Currently every room and its contents suit her perfectly, but as her family grows and changes no doubt the home will slowly grow and change as is required to suit them.

ABOVE
Although it was acquired for her previous home, this chest of drawers fits well in Sam's current bedroom. An early adopter of sustainably sourced items, Sam always seeks out stores with good eco-credentials and her bedroom furniture came from West Elm, one of the first big home retailers to offer fair-trade furnishings.

LEFT
A happy hotchpotch of fashion and beauty accessories cluster together on Sam's dressing table. Hair accessories, perfumes, candles, cosmetics and pretty bags contribute a charming clutter of shapes and colours and offer an element of fun.

OPPOSITE
Sam's calm bedroom has a sleek, tailored style and the clean, simple shapes and warm grey walls are enlivened with a few well-chosen vibrant mustard accents. Retro and quirky accessories add personality to the mix here. The space has a slightly more masculine feel but there are still touches of soft pink and grey to link it back to the other rooms in the house.

I LOVE YOU
TOO HONEY BUNNY
- Pulp Fiction

1970

"Although she likes to take note of new interiors trends, Sam says that sustainability and slow interiors are a high priority."

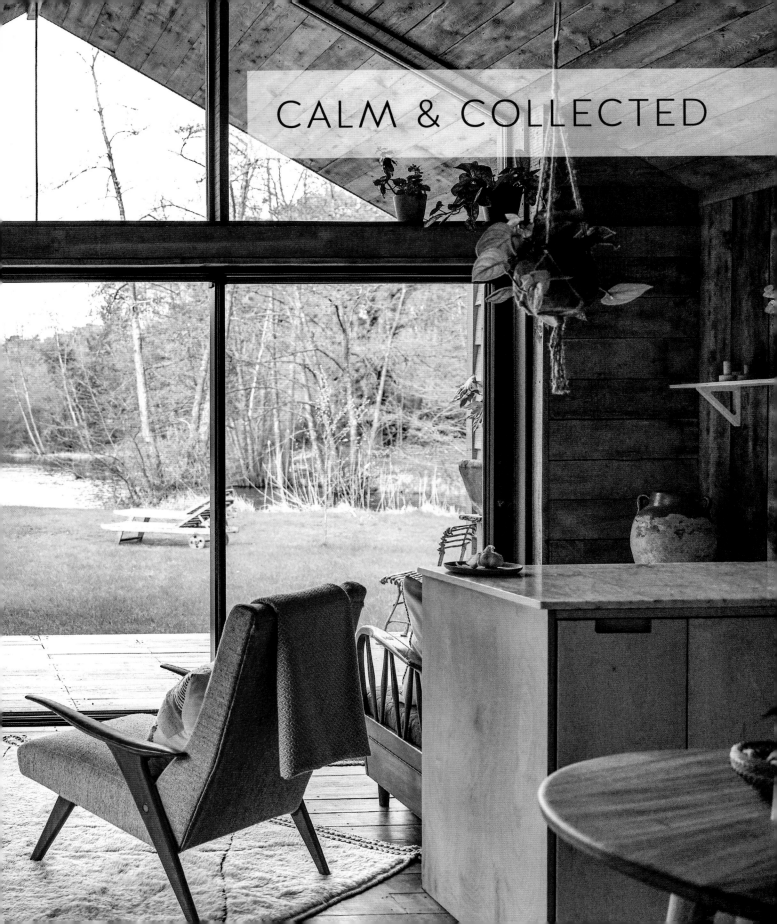

CALM & COLLECTED

CONTENTED
cabin

Jo Moorfoot's lovely lakeside cabin
features a multitude of honest and
humble reclaimed resources and has
been designed to nestle within its
wonderful woodland setting.

An idyllic getaway from the busy hustle and bustle, Jo
Moorfoot's calm contemporary cabin offers visitors the
perfect place to settle down and switch off. Sited beside
a lake on a family-owned 30-acre plot, the cabin is
surrounded by ancient woodland as well as younger trees
that Jo's husband planted as a boy. It's just one of the
places to stay at Settle, a woodland retreat in Norfolk that
Jo runs with her husband John. The concept behind the
whole site as well as this cabin was a desire to get back to
nature and create a destination that offers a respite from
our often busy and hectic modern lives.

As a starting point, Jo and her husband thought about
what they most enjoy doing when getting away from it
all, and this provided inspiration for both the design and
styling of the property. The couple wanted to facilitate
a sense of complete relaxation and create a place that
would allow its inhabitants time to reflect and enjoy being
in the present moment. The landscape setting also played

RIGHT
A U-shaped kitchen occupies one corner of the main living
space, with a peninsula unit facing into the room and the
glorious views beyond. Installing an Ikea frame and cabinets,
the couple added birch ply doors and sourced an old marble
slab for the worksurface, resizing it to fit. Mirroring the clean
lines, a modern table allows for intimate dining.

a large part in the design. The couple wanted to provide a connection with nature in every part of the cabin and there is a deliberate blurring of the boundaries between inside and out. The interior is open plan and the huge floor-to-ceiling windows offer an abundance of natural daylight and glorious lakeside views.

Most of the building materials were reclaimed. John owns a reclamation yard, so the cabin boasts many salvaged features and offered a new lease of life to items that might otherwise have been sent to landfill. Wood from an old hall lines the walls, a glulam beam from a local swimming pool acts as a central support across the roof, old cast-iron radiators keep the interior toasty and an old marble

counter has been reinvented as the kitchen worksurface. Even the cabinetry and unseen materials such as the insulation were made from reclaimed materials. But there are plenty of elegant modern elements here too, such as the huge glazed doors, matt black taps/faucets and a decadent egg-shaped bathtub. These simple yet luxurious touches elevate the experience of being in the cabin.

The colour palette here is almost incidental. It's drawn from the shades and undertones of the reclaimed materials and wooden cladding that form the fabric of the building. Rather than paint the walls, the honeyed shades and intriguing grain of the wood take centre stage and Jo and John made sure that any new items were sourced

OPPOSITE

Sourcing reclaimed wood helped minimize the cabin's environmental footprint. The vintage timber planks bring a wonderfully welcoming feel with their worn and weathered surface. Signs of nail damage and wear and tear contribute to a wonderfully detailed pattern and patina.

ABOVE

There is something immensely appealing about homewares made with warm-to-touch materials. Jo's collection of wooden plate and bowls have artisan but sturdy good looks. Displayed on open shelving, they invite the onlooker to pick them up and handle them.

ABOVE RIGHT

Jo displays dried flowers to add tranquil touches. Here, stems of dried honesty have been arranged with feathery grasses, allowing the intricate and delicate structures to be admired.

RIGHT

Jo chose wall shelving for display and storage. From sustainable companies Woodchuck and Rowan & Wren, the shelves are made from FSC-certified wood and complement the raw wood wall behind.

Taking into account the wonderful lake views right in front of the cabin, the couple sourced cosy yet still flexible seating options to allow for plentiful lounging and viewing. This retro couch has been dressed with cushions and a throw, while the space beneath holds two pouffes that can double as footstools or be used as additional seating.

in similar hues. The end result is hugely appealing, both warm and inviting seen from inside or out.

The cabin interior is calm with little clutter or visual noise, so as not to detract from the sensational views. The handmade birch ply kitchen cabinets are sleek and handleless, narrow shelving offers unobtrusive storage and internal doors glide into purposely crafted recesses. While there are homely touches and tactile accessories, these are tonally coloured or fashioned from organic materials to blend with the background.

The couple found the second-hand furniture and accessories from local auctions and sales. Items are predominantly made from wood, and there is a satisfying blend of vintage and mid-century styles, a nod to modern Scandi rustic styling and a touch of Asian influence in the form of the cane and woven details. Despite the harmonizing tonal shades, different textures prevent the interior from feeling too matchy-matchy and

OPPOSITE
The simple pleasure of uncomplicated, unhurried living is at the heart of Jo and John's woodland retreat. Natural finishes connect the cabin interior to the outside, while the huge glazed doors fill the room with forest scenery. Kindling and dried leaves foraged from the woodland floor have been brought inside to fuel the contemporary wood-burning stove.

Designed expressly for peace and relaxation, the lone bedroom is partitioned off at the back of the cabin. The room has been purposely styled to feel like a snug hideaway with only a notion of what is going on outside glimpsed through the narrow window. A hefty sliding door shuts off this cocooning space from the world beyond, making it a perfect setting for a good night's sleep.

give a sense of longevity to the scheme. There are rough organic finishes thrown into relief by smooth, sanded surfaces. Rumpled linen bedding is perfectly paired with flatweaves and rough-hewn logs are piled high beside the sleek modern wood burning stove. Hand-turned bowls, coarse baskets and chunky ceramics are complemented by refined weaves and delicate glassware. A little garden of potted plants brings nature indoors and softens the cabin's woody interior, making it feel more relaxed and organic. Eco-friendly principles are at the heart of everything that Jo and John do, and the couple have even sourced sustainably made organic candles, soap and toiletries.

At Settle, Jo has successfully created a space that encourages off-grid living. The relaxed good looks and simple interior styling make for a place where you want to down tools, unwind and daydream the time away.

ABOVE LEFT
Ingenious pocket doorways allow unobstructed flow in the small space. Sliding into the thickness of the wall space rather than opening on hinges, the internal doors were all custom-made from reclaimed wood.

ABOVE RIGHT Along the top of the bedroom partition, strip lights have been fitted to gently lift and illuminate the interior. In this darker, more secluded space, shafts of light cast through the narrow window lift the scheme with soulful stillness.

RIGHT & OPPOSITE

The bathroom is the perfect spot for private moments contemplating the beauty of the natural world. Designed with luxury in mind, the handsome egg-shaped bathtub is positioned in the middle of the room, in front of a floor-to-ceiling window that allows bathers to take in the lakeside views. A linen curtain screens the window when necessary. Vintage lighting adds an elegant touch and well-tended plants establish a spa-type mood.

BELOW & BELOW RIGHT

The cabin's huge glass sliding doors and the deep covered porch blur the boundary between indoors and out. At one side, a modest potting table is topped with a salvaged water trough from a farm and displays an impromptu arrangement of plants. On the grass in front of the cabin, a vintage table and folding chairs offer a spot to contemplate the lake beyond and eat al fresco when the weather allows.

"There are elegant modern elements here too, such as the huge glazed sliding doors and a decadent egg-shaped tub."

The focal point of many daily activities, the table and benches add warmth to the white dining area. The table combines FSC-sourced oak and iron in a smart blend of natural and industrial design. Find a similar style at Heals.

PURE *& simple*

Olga Turner Baker and husband Jonathan Baker have created a health-enhancing and relaxing home based on principles of wellbeing. Welcome to their simple, serene and self-restoring sanctuary.

RIGHT
Demonstrating that storecupboard contents can offer a decorative display as well as a practical feature, the couple chose a glazed unit to store herbs and spices and other dry goods. The wooden crates are a practical and stylish way to contain clutter and oddments.

ABOVE
The vintage Ercol chairs were sourced and repainted by the couple using air-purifying Airlite paint, thus adding both a personal and health-enhancing touch.

For design duo Olga and Jonathan, healthy and sustainable home-making is a cause close to their hearts, with wellbeing at the heart of their design consultancy Ekkist. The couple not only run a pioneering practice creating health-enhancing homes, but they have also put their beliefs into practice in their own home, a 1970s house inherited from Jonathan's grandmother.

Most of the couple's design principles are based upon a complex but proven natural synergy between wellbeing and our environment that's supported by extensive scientific and medical research. A careful balance of light, carbon emissions, air purity, water quality and engagement with nature can enhance our living conditions. Accordingly, when they moved to their new home they reconfigured and decorated the three-storey house in their signature 'less-is-more' style. Health-boosting features and eco-friendly finishes abound, as do a multitude of simple ideas that all add up to a very modern way of living.

The couple removed internal walls in order to give every room at least two windows, flooding the interior with stimulating natural daylight that helps to balance circadian rhythms. The pale colour scheme reflects the light and the wall surfaces are finished with breathable mineral paint, which is free of toxic chemicals and

harmful emissions. Olga even made natural air purifiers from left-over paint, which she dried in ice cube trays and has scattered in bowls throughout the house.

Wherever possible, natural wood finishes were chosen for their well-documented calming benefits. Planning regulations meant that new fire doors had to be installed, but even these were responsibly sourced. The couple installed tactile finishing touches around the home, such as a wooden handrail on the staircase with feature stud work crafted by Jonathan. Finished in pure linseed oil, it is warm and pleasing to the touch.

In an effort to reuse what was already in place, the kitchen was freshened up with a coat of eco-friendly paint. Offcuts from the counter tops were mounted on the walls as a splashback and the existing counters were matched with newer sections to more practical effect. Open shelving holds glass jars of dry goods, teas and infusions, bringing natural colours and textures to the space. This is not just a decorative feature: the couple actively avoid plastic and prefer to shop in stores offering refill schemes.

Reinventing and being creative with furniture is a hallmark of Olga and Jonathan's home. Repainting pieces, mixing old and new items, and bringing together different styles,

ABOVE
Orderly arrangements such as this one are pleasing on many levels. Olga and Jonathan's wooden wall shelves feature neat rows of frequently used kitchenwares and foodstuffs. Arranged in this manner, these modest everyday items not only feel more special and cherished but also bring a satisfying feeling of balance and harmony.

OPPOSITE
A monochrome scheme has transformed the existing kitchen. Rather than rip it out and cause unnecessary waste, Olga and Jonathan tweaked the layout and added details in order to make the space work for them. Extra units and worktops were sourced to match what was already there, then all the elements were tied together with a fresh lick of paint and new handles. Airlite paint has been used throughout and an under-sink filter fitted to purify the mains water supply.

such as mid century and vintage, contributes to the relaxed, uncontrived feel. Olga went on an upholstery course to learn how to re-cover Jonathan's grandmother's beloved antique chairs – learning a new skill made them feel personal to her too. As well as reupholstering old chairs, the recycled wood tables and bedside tables/nightstands were made by Olga's father. Older pieces of furniture emit fewer toxic fumes, so are a wise choice if air quality is a consideration. They can also bring the satisfaction of using a family heirloom. Any new pieces of furniture are simple in style and blend in rather than standing out, allowing older items to take centre stage.

Once the bigger decorative decisions were ticked off the list, the couple's sustainable and considered approach was applied to furnishings and fabrics. Natural textiles were integrated into the scheme and the bedlinen bears Oeko-Tex credentials. When it came to bedding, soft-to-the-touch natural fibre fillings were sourced, not only for their eco-values, but also to promote better sleeping patterns.

Olga and Jonathan subscribe to biophilic principles, which suggest that humans are programmed to seek connection with nature, and their home is filled with an abundance of plants and flowers as well as artworks that take

RIGHT
The sitting room is a hive of inspiring elements that all come together creatively. Wherever possible, vintage furniture, retro lighting and heirloom textiles have been used to strike a familiar note as well as making newer buys feel more settled. Carefully sourced conversation pieces add charm and character and shape this personal retreat.

OPPOSITE & RIGHT
The downstairs colour scheme has been continued into the first-floor living room, with similar shades creating a harmonious and comforting look across the home. Eco-friendly linen features on the sofa and footstool. This room also boasts an Awair monitor that tracks air quality and emissions, providing information on chemicals and dust particles.

In a minimalist home, surfaces and textures play an important part in softening each space. In the bedroom, fabrics and bedlinens were chosen for cosy comfort, with quilted covers, velvety cushions, furry rugs and an upholstered headboard.

"Any new pieces of furniture are simple in style and have been chosen to blend in rather than stand out, allowing older items to take centre stage."

nature as their subject matter, many of them by Christabel Forbes. Growing plants indoors, views of greenery, pictures of the natural world, and living with plants all brings us closer to the seasons as well as having proven psychological health benefits.

The couple have also addressed the balance of air- and water-borne toxins with purification devices such as carbon filters on the taps/faucets and hi-tech air

ABOVE
A DIY project such as reupholstering old furniture can bring incredible satisfaction. The process of making is known to have many positive benefits for our mental health.

BELOW
Vibrant artworks adds a welcoming pop of colour in this low-key home. A floating shelf enables them to be arranged in groups themed by colour or subject matter rather than scattered throughout the space, adding impact but in a restrained manner.

FAR LEFT & LEFT
Olga and Jonathan are passionate about the health-giving benefits of living with plants so it's no surprise to find that their bathroom is something of a green oasis, where dainty patterned dishes line up with potted houseplants. This space is usually an area of high humidity so many plants will thrive here even if you don't have green fingers. A maidenhair fern (far left) adds an elegant note with its lacy fronts, while more exotic species add a luxury spa vibe.

filters. However, even simple steps such as adding charcoal sticks to water, choosing air-purifying plants like aloe vera or jade plant, or being able to open windows can also improve the immediate environment. Olga and Jonathan's home shows how conscious choices and even small tweaks can contribute to creating a home that is beautiful, functional and sustainable as well as a joy to live in.

RIGHT
Fresh flowers are a lovely touch in a room and these ones placed by the bedside are a wonderful first sight upon waking. Pick garden offerings or purchase in-season blooms from local shops and markets.

OPPOSITE
In the bathroom, pale marble-effect tiling is broken up by a backsplash made from carefully selected eco-friendly Fired Earth encaustic tiles. Featuring a hand-painted design in calming, aquatic shades, they enliven this simple, peaceful space.

OPPOSITE
In the kitchen, raw wood cabinets in a blond hue add rustic warmth and soften the bold contrasts of the moody walls and clean white tiles. There's plenty of space here for display, storage and food prep stations, all of them framed by the oversized chimneybreast

RIGHT & BELOW RIGHT
Inheriting the tiled floor when she moved into the house, Anneke decided to keep it. A reminder of times gone by, the patterned tiles lend a homely touch with their tonal tessellation and well-used patina.

HUMBLE *beginnings*

Anneke Herbers has drawn on her love for rustic simplicity and the modern aesthetic of Belgian interiors to create a cosy, peaceful home for her family.

Rustic yet sophisticated at the same time, Anneke Herbers' home has a tranquil ambiance. The house was originally Anneke's parents' home, but back in 2000 her father invited Anneke's daughter Marjon to move in to help him keep and breed horses in the paddocks and stables at the rear of the property. Eventually Anneke joined them to be close to her family.

Anneke has always been involved with the world of interiors and styling – she sourced and sold homewares from her previous home and has honed her style over the past 30 years – but she says it was only after taking on this house that she established her unique decorative style. She and Marjon now run Herbers Lifestyle, a popular homewares store in the

LEFT

There are many bespoke finishing touches and details throughout, such as this old gate that has been reused as a door to the pantry. It was cleaned and polished and the central monogram was added by Anneke's husband, making it very special to her.

RIGHT

Large glazed French doors bring atmosphere to the dining area, which has a monumental wood table that can seat up to twelve. Natural daylight pours in, casting long shadows over the floor. Come the night-time, two oversized pendants cast their glow and draw the eye.

"Anneke's passion for Belgian interiors plays a part in this interior. She's a long-time admirer of the style, which is refined and elegant but also relaxed."

nearby town of Valthermond. Anneke says that when she moved in, the property resembled a cabin from the outside, while the interior was old fashioned and full of inherited pieces that were tricky to work with. Anneke stripped the house back to its bare bones and started afresh, while trying to be mindful of how her parents had once lived in and used the home.

Anneke's signature rustic style is an earthy, unpolished look that's just right for where she lives. Signs of the passing seasons have a role to play here, and a connection with nature is evident in the materials she has chosen for the interior. There are cosy spaces that draw people together to linger over meals or settle in for the night. The house radiates textural delights, from the tactile, chalky paints on the walls to the warm, grainy wooden flooring, etched marble details and soft, rumpled linens.

In keeping with Anneke's
favoured Belgian interior
style, oversized furniture
and rustic details make
a statement in the living
room. The handsome,
shapely pieces are given
plenty of space to breathe.
The wooden artwork
hanging on the wall above
the sofa mimics the size,
shape and patterns of the
coffee table (opposite).

Anneke's passion for Belgian interiors also plays a part in this interior. She's a long-time admirer of this style, which is refined and elegant yet relaxed and restrained. Taking its cue from Belgian designers, the decor here is clean-lined and simple yet warm and cosy.

Designed with open-plan living in mind, there is a cohesive feel to Anneke's interior scheme. The same colours and textures reappear throughout, with zones demarcated largely by different pieces of furniture.

In keeping with Anneke's style, most are large in scale and indicate the main function of each and every area. Anneke is part of a tight-knit family, so her home is very much a social space but it also boasts plenty of nooks and crannies for quiet reflection and time out.

A natural palette features throughout. Inspired by the colours of the surrounding landscape and the materials and fabric of her home, Anneke has brought the outdoors inside, using shades of peat, clay and sun-baked reeds

BELOW

Anneke's white-painted bedroom is a tranquil, light-flooded space. Bedlinen, throws, wall colours and accessories continue the pale theme but wooden furniture and flooring prevents the styling from looking cold or austere. Wood brings organic texture too, and links the room back to nature.

alongside lots of hewn timber. Dark spruce velvet and plaster pink linen cover the living room sofas. Mossy greenery is gathered in understated arrangements, while flowers and foliage are placed in pots and planters.

There is a low-key level of pattern evident here, most of it contributed by the natural textures of woven textiles. Subtle decoration also appears in the form of embroidered details, decorative metalwork and antique carvings. In the main, plains prevail, with further interest coming from the patterns thrown by natural light and shade. Lamps and electric illumination are kept to a minimum. As frequently seen in Northern European homes, candles are a popular addition and are dotted throughout, adding homeliness and warmth as and where needed.

Anneke enjoys the making process, and much of the interior is down to her 'can-do' DIY approach – she was responsible for much of the decorating, be it plastering or painting. Her home features many unique touches and details, from the application of clay paints to upcycled finds, including a beautiful wrought-iron gate personalized with her initial by Anneke's husband. The house is filled with artisan-crafted pieces, each with its own story about how it was made, recycled and created.

This home successfully brings together confident styling, natural colours and a sense of togetherness and companionship. Anneke has used sophisticated creative concepts to create an open-hearted home full of intriguing textures, finishes and lighting. It's a delight to live in, and will age with grace and poise.

ABOVE

In the bathroom, Anneke has created a small wet room by building a narrow wall to screen off the shower area. This does away with the need for a curtain or door, retaining the minimal, uncluttered look of the interior.

ABOVE RIGHT

Anneke covered the bathroom and washroom walls herself using Tadelakt, a traditional Moroccan waterproof plaster. The application is labour-intensive, requiring a paste of lime plaster to be polished and treated with soap, but it imparts a beautiful tactile finish rather like polished marble. Anneke added grey pigment when the plaster was applied. It brings warmth to the walls and catches the light exquisitely.

RIGHT

Anneke has used mirrors very cleverly in the smaller rooms. The bathroom could have felt cramped and confined had it not been for the addition of two oversized mirrors. They replicate the effect of windows as well as bouncing much-needed light back into the space.

ABOVE & TOP RIGHT

A new family space has recently
been converted from what was
originally a garage and is linked
to the main building via a corridor.
During the winter months, it offers
the family additional space beyond
the confines of home. In the
summer, the large metal-framed
doors can be thrown open onto
the garden and fields beyond.

RIGHT & OPPOSITE

The styling of this new space is
sympathetic to the rest of Anneke's
home but with a more rustic feel.
It's somewhere the family can spend
time together cooking, eating and
entertaining. Exposed brick and
concrete plaster make up the fabric
of the building and it is furnished
with salvaged pieces, relaxed linens
and handmade ceramics.

HOMEBODY

RIGHT & BELOW

The existing kitchen was moved to the bright new kitchen extension/addition, where it was remodelled and repainted and a new countertop was fitted. The simple open shelving suits the utilitarian, pared-back mood and works better than wall cupboards, which would block the light.

OPPOSITE

A warm grey paint shade has been used throughout Marion's home. The walls have a chalky, matt finish and tone perfectly with the similar low-sheen shade that was chosen for the woodwork/trim.

TIME-HONOURED
style

Taking a slow approach, Marion Visser has given her family home a gradual redesign to create a place where memories of childhood mesh perfectly with present-day moments.

Not many of us are given the chance to live in a home that's been in the family for many years, but this was exactly the opportunity that arose for Marion Visser when she inherited the house that her grandparents built and where she, her father and her siblings all started out in life. The modest home is filled with a sense of family history and shared stories, yet in its current incarnation it is also very much a reflection of Marion's own personality and sense of style.

The current open-plan interior is very different to the property's original layout and use. At the time it was built in 1902, this small two-storey Dutch townhouse housed the whole family downstairs while the upper floor would have been used to store vegetables. Since Marion moved in, the

house has been extended both upwards and outwards to create an additional master bedroom, kitchen and garden room.

The design and flow of the new layout attempts to balance the way Marion uses the space today with an awareness of the building's humble origins. Although the interior has been opened up to suit modern living, she has made sure to retain cosy nooks and corners. Staircases have been turned to align with anterooms and linking spaces opened out to offer seating areas while still taking into account the original footprint of the building. In the attic, space under the eaves has been turned into cupboards. The kitchen units are part of the old home, and where walls have been removed traces of their original positions are still evident, while

OPPOSITE

Marion has chosen not to alter this part of the kitchen. An inset seating area that she remembers fondly from her childhood, it's still one of her favourite spots. The furniture might have changed but the walls still provide a familiar sense of comfort after all these years and it's a reminder of happy family times.

ABOVE

While a kitchen is mostly a practical space, it can also be a lovely place to sit and enjoy the warmth and company. A snug armchair offers a welcome perch for cosy catchups.

LEFT

Seasonal ingredients are appreciated here for their texture and shape and create a simple but pleasing still life.

LEFT

Using reclaimed elements brings character to new settings. Marion fell in love with these salvaged doors long before she knew exactly where she would use them. Rubbed down and painted, they now gracefully line up with the living room walls.

RIGHT

The living room is where television time happens. However, to avoid technology dominating the decor, Marion devised a roomy corner cupboard that houses all wires, routers and screens so the room can remain pared back and calm.

Marion's childhood bunk seat has been given pride of place in the new layout.

Great attention has been paid to finding and reusing older fittings and features so the interior is in keeping with the home's past. Reclaimed planks that originally lined local canals have been repurposed throughout as shelving and storage. Old doors were salvaged to create the built-in storage that conceals essential cabling, wires and modern technology.

A gentle colour palette fluidly links the rooms together, with natural shades of smoke, slate and grey-green used throughout on walls, drapes and upholstery. The accent colours – the dull brown of the wooden floors, moody purple

LEFT

Retained from the house remodel, this internal glazed window allows light to flow through the rooms and connects the old and the new parts of the building.

throws and charcoal kitchenware – offer a gentle tonal side-step from the grey palette. The chalk paint on the walls seems to constantly change hue in the differing light, while its matt finish has an earthy, tactile appeal.

Nature was the inspiration for the choice of wall colours and the changing seasons also have a role to play.

Carefully selected treasures are always on display – a blossoming branch, a cluster of mossy twigs or a handful of dried foliage or seedheads. These natural treasures are a subtle nod to what's happening in the natural world, allowing Marion to appreciate the passing months and the ebb and flow of the seasons.

"Marion has blended old and new as well as simple and sophisticated looks to create a cosy and contemplative home."

Of particular note here is the artful blend of different textures and tactile surfaces. The wonderful chalky walls have already been noted, while the varied textiles offer a sophisticated juxtaposition of the modest and the luxurious. Rich velvets and nubbly woollens are draped alongside hardworking wool, while rough linens have been used to upholster furniture and dress the beds. All materials are of natural origin – there's a ban on plastics and artificial fibres here, in line with Marion's appreciation of the organic and naturally grown.

Marion buys what she loves and what will last, and has incorporated carefully selected antique and vintage pieces.

ABOVE & OPPOSITE

Marion has a masterly touch when it comes to combining different textures to enliven and relieve the simple, sometimes almost monastic backdrop of her home. Shaggy sheepskin throws, plush velvet and washed linens offer a contrast to the dark walls and wide wooden floorboards. The soft furnishings provide a variety of cosy, inviting touchpoints.

OPPOSITE

A favourite space, the garden room is part of the new extension. There are large windows and French doors on two sides of the room, offering uninterrupted garden views.

ABOVE

Practical objects have been used for unassuming displays. Many of them are farm tools showing signs of heavy use or old house fittings and fixtures such as banisters, plinths and pillars. Arranged and presented out of context, they contribute a simple unpretentious individuality.

RIGHT

Dappled sunshine adds abstract patterns as it shines into the garden room. Marion decided not to use curtains or drapes on many of the windows, instead allowing daylight to flood in; sometimes bright and dazzling, at other times moody and atmospheric.

Many of them are flea market finds or were discarded by others. She either accepts these pieces as they are or gives them a new lease of life with a coat of paint or polish, a distressed finish or some decorative detailing. Many of the finds are of humble or practical origin but in Marion's home a table trestle or turned stair balusters are revered just as much as a statue or other artwork.

Marion has blended old and new as well as simple and sophisticated looks to create a cosy and contemplative home. The space perfectly suits her needs, and also brings a treasured family backdrop into the present day, the end result being one that will last the test of time.

ABOVE

Marion's bedroom is in the newly extended loft. In keeping with the rest of her home, it's a quiet and tranquil space but she uses simple seasonal touches to ring the changes. These freshly cut tulips are the perfect example - they brighten a quiet corner and their colour strikes a bright, joyful note amid the subtle warm grey interior.

OPPOSITE

Textures are an essential part of any soulful home. The drape and handle of fabric and its flow and folds brings instant luxury, comfort and calm. Marion has dressed her bedroom simply, but by layering different bedding materials and using heavy drapes at the windows she has brought a stylish and sophisticated mood to this low-ceilinged loft space.

MAKING
memories

Filled with hand-crafted details, Carla Rossiter's perfectly imperfect home is a recycler's dream, brimming with inventive design ideas.

LEFT
A dresser/hutch make take up a lot of space, but it will also provide plenty of useful storage. Carla chose to paint over the original dark wood of this dresser with what she calls 'chippy' paint, bringing character and interesting texture to the piece. Due to its light shade and distressed finish, the dresser/hutch blends in despite its size and boxy shape.

One look around Carla Rossiter's home and it's hard to envisage the decor she describes when she originally took the house on. Carla, not one to shy away from a project, bought the Victorian terraced property despite its ugly woodchip wallpaper, avocado bathroom suite and uninspiring carpets. She could see beyond them to the house's raw potential, had a good feeling about the space and an inkling that it would allow her and her family to create a home true to themselves.

RIGHT
The kitchen extension/addition was created from discarded bricks, many of them found in skips/dumpsters on local streets. Collecting enough was quite an endeavour and it took Carla some time. The end result both saved money and kept materials out of landfill.

The beauty of Carla's home is that nothing has been sourced to match. Assorted inherited and found pieces have been painted or sanded down to connect them to her look, but their differing shapes, styles, heights and materials lend an informal and relaxed look to each room.

Even if something is not in keeping with her style, if it is useful then Carla will work with it. Styled up with a supersized throw, sheepskins and plump cushions, an old sofa is transformed and provides a comfy couch that's large enough for all the family to share.

BELOW & RIGHT

Carla has included many clever and innovative display ideas throughout her home. Different rooms offer different possibilities. In the sitting room, large glass vases hold twigs beside the fireplace, a couple of small tables make for a temporary display that's currently showcasing a cluster of plants, the narrow mantelpiece showcases small treasures and the niche beside the chimneybreast has been transformed by shelving and a reclaimed wooden backdrop. A mirror that once belonged to Carla's father's takes pride of place on one shelf, reflecting all these charming decorative details.

The house underwent two phases of renovation. The first was a gradual process of making a home of the new space and the second was a kitchen and loft extension/addition as the family grew. Carla is not one to slavishly follow trends and creating a home to suit her family was her main aim during the process.

Throughout the interior, a calm, neutral colour palette acts as a gentle backdrop to multiple textural finishes. Carla made her own chalky paint using leftover paint and experimented by painting it onto all sorts of surfaces, even soft furnishings. The result is a relaxed, homely space adorned with pared-down pieces and family treasures.

Carla admits to having a love of recycling and repurposing and her constant scouting for raw materials and quirky finds is a lifelong hobby

that is evident everywhere in her home. Almost everything here has enjoyed a previous life or has been repaired or repurposed into something new. Many items were discovered in skips/dumpsters or found on the side of the street and given a new lease of life. Carla finds beauty in an item's knocks and bumps, believing that they only add to the history of a piece. The kitchen island, for example, was fashioned from a dressing table that had been abandoned by the side of the road, old floorboards were used as wall cladding and shelving, and the kitchen extension was borne from an admirable endeavour of collecting and reusing old, unwanted bricks – a mission which has brought an interesting talking point to the space as well as keeping the bricks out of landfill.

Sustainable and eco-aware ideas influence how Carla's family live in their home. Specially sourced sustainable Tencel bed linen made from eucalyptus pulp was chosen over cotton, they use bamboo toothbrushes and most of the glassware is recycled or second hand. Reducing single-use plastic consumption, hand-making cleaning products, passing on unwanted possessions, and hand-crafting gifts and seasonal decorations are part of everyday life here.

ABOVE LEFT
Carla's creative can-do approach means there are many enviable hand-crafted pieces dotted around her home, including a retro-style lampshade that was looking tired until Carla updated it with some intricate hand embroidery.

ABOVE RIGHT
In order to make the best use of space in the home office, many of the fittings were custom-built (also see opposite). Rather than a bulky shop-bought desk, a slim worksurface has been installed beneath the window. The alcove beside the chimneybreast is home to a useful drawers-cum-shelf unit while work tidies are neatly tucked in below.

Rethinking an item's use is second nature for Carla. She removed the handles from some old drawers then stacked them against the wall to create a display unit. Carla painted the bottom of some of the drawers for a bold geometric effect.

Of particular note is the number of what can only be described as 'have a go' ideas. These feature throughout, ranging from practical DIY jobs such as plastering to more unusual crafty details such as mosaic making, appliqué, crochet and bespoke mirror distressing. Carla has gained huge satisfaction from these tasks, and says the jobs that require most effort are often the ones that turn out to be the most rewarding. Her 'make do and mend' mindset is inherited from her family, with her father being her upcycling role model. Carla has fond memories of watching him turn something trivial into a treasured item, and now uses his tools to craft her own objects. There are many other inherited heirlooms and quirky features that spark happy memories. Her grandfather's painted chair revealed all sorts of colourful past decorating trends when

One new buy was Carla's bathtub, but it has been given a lived-in look thanks to a couple of panels made from distressed floorboards. The bathroom is a pared-back space, so Carla added a delicate flourish to the window by making a simple blind then appliquéing it with vintage doilies.

BELOW LEFT

Skip/dumpster and street finds have been upcycled into ingenious storage solutions throughout Carla's home. Here, an old metal and wood shelving unit has been installed in a corner of the bathroom to display a collection of houseplants. The wooden doors have been given a light coat of chalky paint that allows the grain to show through. On the back of the door, a row of swivelling hooks are a home for robes and towels.

BELOW RIGHT

Elsewhere in the bathroom, two traditional-style basins have been positioned side by side for 'his and hers' ablutions. Vintage finds, such as the two slightly mismatching medicine cabinets, soften the subway tiling and sanitaryware.

RIGHT

Repurposed floorboards are a signature element throughout Carla's home Here they hide pipework in the bathroom, but elsewhere they have been made into shelving and storage units or used to clad the walls and provide backdrops to shelves or alcoves, where they add texture and character.

RIGHT & FAR RIGHT

There are many sentimental keepsakes and mementoes in Carla's home. Some are inherited and others found or foraged in the everyday course of life. Bringing texture and detail to a room, many of them are presented in unique ways or recall special people or places. Here a photograph printed on a feather is an unusual way of remembering a loved one, while the preserved flowers keep the passing seasons fresh in the mind.

LEFT & OPPOSITE

Many of the walls in this home have been given character with textural effects. Carla created the finish on the bedroom walls, which resembles elegantly distressed plasterwork, by applying coats of homemade chalk paint to the walls and painstakingly smudging, ragging and stippling to achieve the desired effect. The result is a beautiful canvas that provides a graceful backdrop for her bedroom furnishings.

"Carla admits to having a love of recycling and repurposing, and her constant scouting for raw materials and quirky finds is a lifelong hobby."

Carla stripped it back, while a vintage mirror that was accidentally distressed by her father now enjoys pride of place. Scratch marks on the kitchen dresser bring back fond memories of Miniature Schnauzer Winnie pawing eagerly at a drawer for treats. The presence of these treasured items reminds Carla of her parents' hotly debated opinions on timeworn paint and patina, which have become something of a long-running family joke.

Nature and the seasons are another recurrent theme. Everywhere you look, there are plants, dried foliage and fallen branches found on family foraging sessions, gleaned from friends' gardens or acquired at community plant swaps. Whether artfully crafted into seasonal wreaths or simply popped into a vase, Carla admits to finding huge enjoyment in seeing natural items in her home and finds the process of preserving fulfilling.

In Carla's world, there is a beauty in even the most modest of finds. The house is full of happy memories and each and every piece has its own unique story, from sourcing to final setting.

FREE SPIRIT

CREATIVE
canvas

A desire to combine family living with her art and craft business has resulted in a beautiful and inviting home for Margo Hupert, one that combines everyday comfort with a versatile and inspiring backdrop.

RIGHT & BELOW
Everyday items bring a homely touch to Margo's modern kitchen, softening the hard edges and bringing subtle touches of colour to the room via their different materials. Arranged on a long wall shelf that stretches the length of the kitchen counter, kitchenware and accessories draw the eye. Practical essentials and handcrafted treasures all jostle together in easy-going clusters.

For artist Margo Hupert, it was essential to create a home that would be able to function smoothly for family life, spark inspiration for her creative career and provide a base for her small but growing company.

Purchased in 2014, the apartment was originally a series of small rooms that Margo combined to provide more spacious living quarters. The kitchen, for example, was repositioned in order to create a free-flowing family and work space. Although the interior is now open plan, there are still plenty of quiet corners for tranquil moments. A chaise longue tucked into a sunny alcove leading off the busy kitchen-diner, for example, is a spot designed

OPPOSITE
Rearranging her plant collection is a particular pleasure for Margo. Inspired by the seasons, she brings sprigs and branches inside to bud and blossom. In springtime, she likes to pot bulbs into special glass vases that display the intricacies of both the flower and its shoots.

ABOVE

The capacious glazed display cabinet in Margo's dining area holds all her glassware and china. Its artfully distressed finish is not limited to the exterior – the inside has also been carefully treated to provide an attractive backdrop for her simple white tableware and elegant glasses.

for relaxation and respite, perfect for five minutes with a morning coffee or winding down with a herbal tea after dinner.

Margo's apartment plays several different roles. As well as a busy family home, it is also a gallery space to showcase her artworks, so the decor required some versatility. The result is warm and welcoming, yet provides something of a blank canvas for ever-changing displays. Margo gave the walls a weathered look, thanks to a selection of water-based paints and bare plaster finishes, and the uninspiring cream colour scheme she inherited on moving in was swiftly replaced by a tranquil neutral palette. Peaceful shades wash over everything from the walls to the floors to linens and textiles. The tall

Raw plaster and similar paint effects are used with great impact on the walls in Margot's home. Not only do they provide her with a variety of different backdrops for her artwork, they also add warmth and character to a room. She's not worried about a perfect finish – bumps, cracks and scuffs are all welcome here.

Margo's eclectic taste encompasses multiple different styles. In her office area, an industrial-style folding table, factory steps and seating, woven rattan lampshades, a vintage cabinet, a plan chest and modern office storage all sit comfortably together. Plants and textiles are used to relax and tone hard edges.

windows are screened with sheer drapes that dapple the natural light and Margo's use of fabric is informal in style, bringing a cosy and relaxed feeling. The soft tones of the decor have the added benefit of bouncing natural daylight around the interior. Floors have a glossy sheen, tiles gleam and the glazed pictures and cabinets and glassware sparkle.

When it came to the furniture and fittings, Margo has mixed global elements with older pieces, many of them revamped or restored by Margo herself. She believes that the process of repairing and redecorating unloved items – stripping them, refinishing them and recovering them with vintage textiles – fosters a special relationship with the pieces. Margo feels the same affection for her homewares. Objects crafted by friends and family are valued above designer finds, with emotional succour drawn from the creativity of loved ones. Functional items sit happily beside special possessions and their unique beauty is admired as much as that of rarer ornaments.

Margo spent much of her childhood in her grandfather's forest home and describes herself as hugely inspired by and connected to nature. It's no surprise that she has chosen to surround herself with greenery and natural objects at home. Plants inspire and feature in her drawings,

ABOVE
Running a company from home can call for alternative storage ideas. Margo uses an old wooden box beneath her desk and a vintage suitcase to hold postal tubes. Their attractive circular forms and warm colour pleasingly echo the natural hues of the lampshades.

"Functional items sit happily beside special possessions, and their humble beauty is admired just as much as that of rarer ornaments."

ABOVE LEFT

The tools of Margo's trade are out on show here, offering an insight into her creativity. Wirework baskets hold paint pots and old jugs store her brushes.

LEFT

Fading flowers give Margo just as much pleasure as their counterparts in full bloom. There is a beauty in the way their colours and characteristics change as they wane and wither. The process of this gradual but inevitable transformation is an intriguing one and watching it connects Margo with nature.

ABOVE & OPPOSITE

The wall behind Margo's computer station is used as a mood board for an array of favourite images. Photographs, postcards and framed pictures provide visual inspiration, while the desk is home to all manner of attractive objects, from candles to antique figurines and a vintage typewriter. A couple of oversized plants add a splash of green and break up the straight lines. It's been proven that some houseplants can absorb electromagnetic radiation so make a great addition to a work station – look for aloe vera, ivy and cacti.

so naturally they play a starring role in every room and are often moved from room to room. There is also a celebration of the changing seasons here, with ever-evolving displays of cut and foraged flowers and foliage. Early spring bulbs and budding branches hold the promise of the warmer months to come, and rather than discarding them once flowering is over, Margo likes to dry the blooms, allowing them to be enjoyed for longer.

Wellbeing has been creatively and consciously addressed in the way the family inhabit their home. The air quality is monitored and purified, with natural candles, oils and diffusers, adding a calming fragrance. The family shop from a community co-op where raw ingredients can be bought in bulk in plastic-free packaging. Once home, items are transferred to handy containers, be they pots, boxes, cases or baskets. There's a noticeable absence of

BELOW & RIGHT

There is little pattern to be found in Margo's choices of fabric and wallpaper designs, perhaps due to the fact that her home partly functions as a gallery space and plain walls offer the most versatile backdrop for artworks. However, there are numerous pretty decorative details and intriguing textures throughout, including the rich patina of vintage furnishings. Plants and flowers in particular are a great way of introducing shape and colour, such as the boldly striped markings of a calathea and the delicate heart-shaped leaves of an oxalis (right).

OPPOSITE

A gentle layering of different textures has created a reposeful bedroom. Diaphanous voile curtains cloak the end wall and even the light fitting is encased in a hessian-type fabric to diffuse the light it throws. The bed linen is simple yet comforting, offering layers of cotton and linen topped with a woollen blanket.

synthetic materials in this home. Surfaces are natural, and the furniture and decorative objects are crafted from wood, rattan and ceramics. Margo's collection of recycled glass jars and planters hold both food and fauna. Seasonal flowers are a favourite feature: spring bulbs grow in glass planters while raw ingredients also provide colour and texture.

Every element in Margo's home has been carefully and consciously chosen. There is so much to inspire here, from the restrained yet tactile decor to Margo's readiness to constantly mix things up and her deep love for and appreciation of the home that she has built.

CULTURE *clash*

A lifelong lover of global looks and monochrome shades, Alexandra van Rennes' home blends rich textures and tones to create an atmospheric and sociable interior.

Choosing to create a home with black walls and floors is not for the faint hearted, but Alexandra van Rennes says sombre backdrops have always been at the heart of her decorating schemes. It's certainly a bold choice, but thanks to splashes of white and layered textures, a balance of light and shade and a carefully chosen array of vintage finds, a homely mood softens the strong features of this dramatic interior.

Originally bought in 2005, the property was purchased to house Alexandra's growing family. She was attracted by the spacious interior and the fact that the house offered a blank canvas, although it lacked the charm and character of her previous home and had little in the way of soft landscaping or planting outside. This scarcity of nature was to have a significant effect on the mood inside the house: Alexandra was determined from the start to bring organic elements inside to give life to her new home.

LEFT
Despite choosing a restricted palette, Alexandra has kept her space interesting by blending contrasting textures. In the kitchen area, varied seating allows family and friends to gather. There are plenty of cosy elements, while the minimalist blinds offer a practical solution to privacy issues.

Despite the austere interior, Alexandra took her time when it came to decorating. Her love of a black and white palette is a signature style that she has developed over the years. However, careful consideration was made when it came to choosing exactly the right shades: she opted for a warm black with a charcoal undertone that perfectly complements the soft, milky white. The resulting monochrome look is classic rather than reliant on passing trends, and for Alexandra this simple but striking scheme has stood the test of time. What's more, using a restricted palette throughout the home allows for a certain flexibility as furniture and accessories can constantly be swapped around as they will fit in anywhere, decoratively speaking.

The house is divided into a large open-plan space downstairs with individual rooms on the upper floor. Dividing the large open area into separate zones while keeping an overall cohesive vibe was a priority. In the living room,

ABOVE
An old window frame has been given a new purpose as a chalkboard and an extra place to pop postcards and store keys A string of bells allows the cook to announce dinner.

RIGHT
Vintage finds and simple everyday tableware bring personality and a lived-in feel to the modern kitchen. The wood cladding above the stove breaks up the monochrome effect, while pendant lights and hanging storage create a division between the kitchen and seating areas. Cosy textures come in the form of rugs, throws and baskets.

OPPOSITE
Alexandra's eye for detail brings charm and life to a scheme. Vintage shoes – a cherished bazaar find – have been mounted inside a carved wooden frame, plump cushions are tossed invitingly on the daybed and the chalkboard is part-practical addition, part-abstract artwork.

"A lover of travel, Alexandra is a consummate souvenir hunter and her pan-global style features woven baskets, bazaar trinkets and flea-market finds."

LEFT & OPPOSITE

The dining area sits between the kitchen and the living room. Here, a vintage moulded plastic chair, rustic wooden benches and other retro seating are drawn up around the modern wood and metal table. As elsewhere, a natural palette of raw wood and woven natural fibres lightens the simple black and white scheme. Alexandra has a knack for using texture to soften harder edges. A washed linen cloth part-covers the table, while dull brass candlesticks and hand-crafted ceramics create a sense of occasion.

light pours through vast windows, filtering through linen blinds and falling onto the different surfaces. Lustrous black floors, glossy furniture, soft velvets and the odd metallic touch gleam and smoulder, while textural elements captivate the eyes in the changing light. The furniture has been carefully positioned to meet the needs of family living. There is plenty of

varied seating to encourage spending time together: a huge modular sofa, a deep rattan daybed, wooden benches and even a hanging chair, all of which are ideal for impromptu gatherings or quiet reading or laptop action. This is one of Alexandra's favourite areas and the family spend much of their time here, chatting, napping or reading.

LEFT

Alexandra's favourite space is the living area. The sleek, low-level L-shaped sofa encloses this area and creates a cosy, cocooning vibe that brings the family together to spend time watching, reading and just hanging out. As you might expect, cushions and textiles proliferate here, while a Moroccan-style rug warms up the tiled floor.

RIGHT

The wood-clad chimney breast is home to an array of casually arranged family photos in assorted frames – a collection that demands a closer look.

It's an inviting space with an open fire and dressed with cosy rugs and cushions. The floor-to-ceiling windows at one end of the space offer panoramic views onto the garden and grassy wilds beyond.

A lover of travel, Alexandra is a consummate souvenir hunter and her pan-global style features woven baskets, bazaar trinkets and flea-market finds. Most things have been used and have a unique history that continues to develop in their current surroundings, adding character and charisma to the home. Signs of use, handling, wear and tear and knocks and scrapes are all appreciated, indeed welcomed, by Alexandra. Displayed in collections, her decorative accessories jostle for space in a 'more the merrier' manner, many of them grouped by type, theme or use.

There is also a casual disregard when it comes to sticking to a particular style or era, so mid-century and antique pieces sit happily next to one another and accept new additions as and when they come along. Old pieces of furniture are regularly given a facelift with a coat of paint rather than being thrown away.

Textures play a starring role here. Alexandra is passionate about nature and its mood-enhancing effects, so for her these textures are

ABOVE LEFT

In the main bedroom, souvenirs brought back from Alexandra's travels have been put on display – treasured reminders of distant travel and exotic destinations. The backs of old canvases, wooden beads, a bleached skull and a bronze figurine all share a warm tonal palette and are showcased by the velvety walls.

ABOVE RIGHT

Too much black and white can feel stark, so Alexandra has opted to use mostly dark hues in this bedroom. As well as the dense, soft black walls she's included other sombre shades such as soft smoke, forest greens and thundery blues.

a way of bringing it inside. Alexandra is not a huge fan of houseplants, but foliage features in the form of dried weaves such as rattan lampshades, matting, wicker seating and baskets, which tone well with the warm wood finishes on walls, furniture and homewares. These organic textures soften the monochrome scheme and add earthy, tactile details.

Gradually growing and maturing alongside the family that inhabits it, Alexandra's home exudes a feel-good manner. Welcoming and inviting, it draws family and friends inside and inspires them to linger, thanks to its comforting style, distinctive charm and original treasures.

OPPOSITE

A black and white scheme can be surprisingly snug and soothing in a bedroom, especially a small one. The black bedhead melts into the walls, drawing attention to the cosy pillows and the photos and prints on the wall shelf, which was painted the same shade as the walls, naturally. The metal pendant lampshade introduces a dull gleam that stands out against the matt surfaces and brightens the space.

SOURCES

FABRICS & TEXTILES

THE AFRICAN FABRIC SHOP
africanfabric.co.uk
Fair trade, responsibly sourced artisan-made batiks, weaves, textiles and cloths. They even source baskets and beads.

BEYOND FRANCE
beyondfrance.co.uk
European vintage and reclaimed textiles and fabrics, including linens, grain sacks and sheeting.

IAN MANKIN
ianmankin.co.uk
Upholstery and curtain fabrics made from natural, recycled and certified organic fibres that are chemical free, supporting the use of sustainable textiles.

LARUSI
larusi.com
Renowned for their Moroccan weaves, rugs and textiles.

LINENME
linenme.com
Sustainably sourced, biodegradable linens. With slow living and consumption considerations, they use surplus fabric off-cuts to avoid waste going to landfill.

LOOM & LAST
loomandlast.com
Natural cottons and linens for bedrooms, drapes and homewares. They use reusable cotton bags as packaging to encourage recycling.

THE ORGANIC COMPANY
organiccompany.dk
Danish company producing bed, bath and kitchen linens and homewares from 100% GOT-certified organic cotton.

URBAN COLLECTIVE
urbancollective.com
Bamboo and organic bedding, cushions and towels.

SURFACES

CAWARDEN BRICK & TILE COMPANY LTD
cawardenreclaim.co.uk
Reclaimed and period building products, from joinery to chimney pots. Less than 1% of on-site waste goes to landfill.

CEMENT TILE SHOP
cementtileshop.com
US supplier of encaustic cement tiles from Europe. Will ship their beautiful tiles all around the world.

FARROW & BALL
farrow-ball.com
Eco-friendly water-based and cruelty free paints with low VOC. Their wallpapers are made from high-quality paper sourced from sustainable forests and manufactured in their Dorset factory.

LASSCO
lassco.co.uk
This unique company provides salvaged exterior and interior antiques, including homewares.

LITTLE GREENE
littlegreen.com
Their wide range of water-based paints have virtually zero VOC content while the paper used for their wallpapers comes from FSC or PEFC certified sustainable areas. Paint tins include 50% recycled steel.

NAKED FLOORING COMPANY
nakedflooring.co.uk
Undyed wool carpets and natural fibre flooring and rugs.

THE NEW & RECLAIMED FLOORING COMPANY
reclaimedflooringco.com
UK- and US-based restored and reclaimed wood flooring and walling company.

FURNITURE & LIGHTING

Adventures in Furniture
aif.london
Lasting pieces made from sustainable materials combined with a company ethos that prioritises carbon offsetting.

ANOTHER COUNTRY
anothercountry.com
Timeless designs inspired by Japanese and Scandinavian styles with an emphasis on sustainability and responsibly sourced timber.

CLEARWATER
clearwaterbaths.com
Natural stone baths made from sustainable materials

COX & COX
coxandcox.co.uk
A beautiful range of rattan pendants handwoven from natural fibres.

POTTERY BARN
A range of sustainably sourced and artisan-made homewares.

RESTORATION HARDWARE
restorationhardware.com
Many of their products are Greenguard certified and artisan-made.

RUST COLLECTIONS
rustcollections.co.uk
Handsome bespoke furniture created individually in the workshop using reclaimed wood from local yards.

TALA
eu.tala.co.uk
Elegant and sustainable LED lighting that reduces energy consumption and carbon dioxide output.

TIKAMOON
tikamoon.com
French brand offering contemporary furniture and fittings, including wicker and bamboo pieces.

TINE K HOME
tinekhome.com
Danish homeware company renowned for their eco-friendly bamboo home furnishings including some beautiful handmade lighting.

THE USED KITCHEN COMPANY
theusedkitchencompany.com
This brand has won many recycling and sustainability awards due to its positive impact on the environment, selling used or ex-display kitchens to avoid them going to landfill.

WEST ELM
Westelm.com
Setting ambitious sustainability and Fair Trade targets, West Elm produce modern furniture and homewares designed to last.

WOODCHUCK
woodchuck.nl
Simple, sublime FSC-certified furniture made in small batches to limit their environmental footprint.

HOMEWARES & WELLBEING

BENTLEY ORGANIC
bentleyorganic.com
Their organic range is environmentally friendly with most items suitable for vegans.

BOHEMIA
bohemiadesign.co.uk/
Traditional crafts from all over the world.

CHALK & MOSS
chalkandmoss.com/
Organic, natural homewares and linens.

DESIGN VINTAGE
designvintage.co.uk
Offering vintage pieces alongside sleek modern homewares.

ECO BATH LONDON
ecobathlondon.com
Natural, organic soaps with packaging made from recycled materials.

I GIGI
igigigeneralstore.com
Vintage finds, handmade wares and an interior design service too.

MAUD AND MABEL
maudandmabel.com
Contemporary crafts grounded in traditional Japanese aesthetics.

NKUKU
nkuku.com/
Nkuku uses waste and recycled goods to make eco-friendly, beautifully designed products.

THE FUTURE KEPT
thefuturekept.com
Ethically sourced and sustainably made products for home and garden.

THE KINDCRAFT
thekindcraft.com
Offers a carefully curated collection of handmade goods and slow fashion.

RELISH
relishlifestyle.co.uk/
Vintage and antique homewares and furniture.

TINCTURE
tincturelondon.com
Gorgeous non-toxic vegan and cruelty-free cleaning products for the home.

URBANARA
urbanara.com
A simple, timeless range of textiles made from recycled materials and natural fibres.

WEARTH LONDON
wearthlondon.com
Eco-friendly products and zero-waste essentials made by ethical independent brands.

WEAVER GREEN
www.weavergreen.com
Rugs and other homewares made from 100% recycled plastic bottles.

PAINTS

AIRLITE
airlite.com
Preventing bacteria and mould from forming within the home, Airlite paints come in a beautiful choice of colours.

ANNIE SLOAN
anniesloan.com
A unique water-based chalky formula that's non-toxic, virtually odour-free and can be applied to most surfaces.

BAUWERK
bauwerkcolour.co.uk
Made from natural materials such as clay, Bauwerk paint is made to non-toxic vegan formulas and uses 100% green power in the production process.

EARTHBORN
earthbornpaints.co.uk
VOC-free paint that are breathable, eco-friendly and safe to use throughout the home.

EDWARD BULMER
edwardbulmerpaint.co.uk
Paints in glorious colours mixed from natural pigments.

GRAPHENSTONE
graphenstone.co.uk
Breathable paints free from toxic substances that absorb CO_2 from the environment.

LAKELAND
lakelandpaints.co.uk
Non-toxic, odourless and solvent free organic paints.

PICTURE CREDITS

KEY: a = above, b = below, r = right, l = left, c= centre.

All photography by Dan Duchars

Endpapers and page 1 The home of illustrator and designer Margo Hupert in Poland, margohupert.pl, @margo.hupert.art; *2* Anneke Herbers and Marjon Herbers, herberslifestyle.nl; *3 left* Anneke Herbers and Marjon Herbers, herberslifestyle.nl; *3c* The London home of Catherine Ashton of @bo_decor; *3r* Settle Norfolk, slow living and boutique cabin, carriages and camping set in a private 30 acre parkland; *4* The London home of Carla Rossiter of @shedhomewares_E17; *5–6* The home of illustrator and designer Margo Hupert in Poland, margohupert. pl, @margo.hupert.art; *7* Settle Norfolk, slow living and boutique cabin, carriages and camping set in a private 30 acre parkland; *8* The home of Marion Visser in the Netherlands of @stoerwonenenleven; *10* Clare Lattin co-founder of DuckSoup and LittleDuck, @lattin72; *11a* The London home of Carla Rossiter of @shedhomewares_E17; *11c* The home of Marion Visser in the Netherlands of @stoerwonenenleven; *11b* The home of illustrator and designer Margo Hupert in Poland, margohupert.pl, @margo.hupert.art; *12a* The London home of Carla Rossiter of @shedhomewares_E17; *12b* Clare Lattin co-founder of DuckSoup and LittleDuck, @lattin72; *13–14* The home of Alexandra van Rennes, petithanout.nl; *15al and bl* The London home of Carla Rossiter of @shedhomewares_E17; *15ar and br* Clare Lattin co-founder of DuckSoup and LittleDuck, @lattin72; *16* The home of illustrator and designer Margo Hupert in Poland, margohupert.pl, @margo.hupert.art; *17* styled by Sara Bird; *18a* The London home of Catherine Ashton of @bo_ decor; *18c* Clare Lattin co-founder of DuckSoup and LittleDuck, @lattin72; *18b* The home of Samantha Thompson in London, @LondonStyleSisters; *19* The home of illustrator and designer Margo Hupert in Poland, margohupert.pl, @margo.hupert.art; *20* The London home of Carla Rossiter of @shedhomewares_ E17; *21a and bl* The London home of Carla Rossiter of @shedhomewares_E17; *21bl and 22* Clare Lattin co-founder of DuckSoup and LittleDuck, @lattin72; *23al* The home of Marion Visser in the Netherlands of @stoerwonenenleven; *23ar* The London home of Catherine Ashton of @bo_decor; *23bl* The home of illustrator and designer Margo Hupert in Poland, margohupert.pl, @margo.hupert.art; *23br* The London home of Catherine Ashton of @bo_decor; *24* Clare Lattin co-founder of DuckSoup and LittleDuck, @lattin72; *25* styled by Sara Bird; *26a* The London home of Catherine Ashton of @bo_decor; *26c* The home of Alexandra van Rennes, petithanout.nl; *26b* The home of Marion Visser in the Netherlands of @stoerwonenenleven; *27* The home of Marion Visser in the Netherlands of @stoerwonenenleven; *28* The home of illustrator and designer Margo Hupert in Poland, margohupert. pl, @margo.hupert.art; *29al* Anneke Herbers and Marjon Herbers, Herberslifestyle.nl; *29ar and b* Settle Norfolk, slow living and boutique cabin, carriages and camping set in a private 30 acre parkland; *30al* Anneke Herbers and Marjon Herbers, Herberslifestyle.nl; *30 ar and cl* The London home of Carla Rossiter of @shedhomewares_E17; *30cr* The home of Marion Visser in the Netherlands of @stoerwonenenleven; *30bl* Anneke Herbers and Marjon Herbers, Herberslifestyle.nl; *30br* The home of illustrator and designer Margo Hupert in Poland, margohupert.pl, @margo.hupert.art; *31* The home of Marion Visser in the Netherlands of @stoerwonenenleven; *32* styled by Sara Bird; *33* The London home of Carla Rossiter of @shedhomewares_E17; *34 and 35a* The home of Marion Visser in the Netherlands of @stoerwonenenleven; *35c* The home of illustrator and designer Margo Hupert in Poland, margohupert. pl, @margo.hupert.art; *35b* The London home of Catherine Ashton of @bo_decor; *36* The home of illustrator and designer Margo Hupert in Poland, margohupert.pl, @margo.hupert.art; *37al* The home of Alexandra van Rennes, petithanout.nl; *37ar* Clare Lattin co-founder of DuckSoup and LittleDuck, @lattin72; *37bl* The home of Alexandra van Rennes, petithanout.nl; *37br* The London home of Catherine Ashton of @bo_decor; *38* The home of Samantha Thompson in London @LondonStyleSisters; *39al* The London home of Carla Rossiter of @shedhomewares_E17; *39ar* Clare Lattin co-founder of DuckSoup and LittleDuck, @lattin72; *39b* The home of Marion Visser in the Netherlands of @stoerwonenenleven; *40* styled by Sara Bird; *41* Anneke Herbers and Marjon Herbers, Herberslifestyle.nl; *42* The London home of Catherine Ashton of @bo_decor; *43a* The home of Marion Visser in the Netherlands of @stoerwonenenleven; *43c* The London home of Catherine Ashton of @bo_decor; *43b* The home of Marion Visser in the Netherlands of @stoerwonenenleven; *44al* The home of Samantha Thompson in London @LondonStyleSisters; *44ar* The home of illustrator and designer Margo Hupert in Poland, margohupert.pl, @margo.hupert.art; *44bl* Clare Lattin co-founder of DuckSoup and LittleDuck, @lattin72; *44br* The home of Samantha Thompson in London @LondonStyleSisters; *45* The home of illustrator and designer Margo Hupert in Poland, margohupert.pl, @margo.hupert.art; *46al and b* Anneke Herbers and Marjon Herbers, Herberslifestyle.nl; *46ar* The London home of Catherine Ashton of @bo_decor; *47* Anneke Herbers and Marjon Herbers, Herberslifestyle.nl; *48* The home of illustrator and designer Margo Hupert in Poland, margohupert.pl, @margo.hupert.art; *49* styled by Sara Bird; *50* Settle Norfolk, slow living and boutique cabin, carriages and camping set in a private 30 acre parkland; *51a* The home of Olga Turner and Jonathan Baker of Ekkist design consultancy; *51c* The home of illustrator and designer Margo Hupert in Poland, margohupert.pl, @margo.hupert.art; *51b* The London home of Catherine Ashton of @bo_decor; *52al* Clare Lattin co-founder of DuckSoup and LittleDuck, @lattin72; *52ar* The home of Samantha Thompson in London @LondonStyleSisters; *52b* The home of illustrator and designer Margo Hupert in Poland, margohupert.pl, @margo.hupert.art; *53* Clare Lattin co-founder of DuckSoup and LittleDuck, @lattin72; *54* Settle Norfolk, slow living and boutique cabin, carriages and camping set in a private 30 acre parkland; *55al and cl* Clare Lattin co-founder of DuckSoup and LittleDuck, @lattin72; *55ar*

Anneke Herbers and Marjon Herbers, Herberslifestyle.nl; *55cr* The home of illustrator and designer Margo Hupert in Poland, margohupert.pl, @margo.hupert.art; *55bl* Settle Norfolk, slow living and boutique cabin, carriages and camping set in a private 30 acre parkland; *55br* Anneke Herbers and Marjon Herbers, Herberslifestyle.nl; *56* styled by Sara Bird; *57* The home of illustrator and designer Margo Hupert in Poland, margohupert.pl, @margo.hupert.art; *58* The London home of Catherine Ashton of @bo_decor; *59* The home of illustrator and designer Margo Hupert in Poland, margohupert.pl, @margo.hupert.art; *60–71* The London home of Catherine Ashton of @bo_decor; *72–81* Clare Lattin co-founder of DuckSoup and LittleDuck, @lattin72; *82–91* The home of Samantha Thompson in London @LondonStyleSisters; *92–112* Settle Norfolk, slow living and boutique cabin, carriages and camping set in a private 30 acre parkland; *104–113* The home of Olga Turner and Jonathan Baker of Ekkist design consultancy; *114–123* Anneke Herbers and Marjon Herbers, Herberslifestyle.nl; *124–137* The home of Marion Visser in the Netherlands of @stoerwonenenleven; *138–147* The London home of Carla Rossiter of @shedhomewares_E17; *148–159* The home of illustrator and designer Margo Hupert in Poland, margohupert.pl, @margo.hupert.art; *160–169* The home of Alexandra van Rennes, petithanout.nl; *171* The London home of Catherine Ashton of @bo_decor; *174* The home of illustrator and designer Margo Hupert in Poland, margohupert.pl, @margo.hupert.art; *176* The London home of Carla Rossiter of @shedhomewares_E17.

INSTAGRAM ACCOUNTS WE LOVE

HOMES FEATURED IN THIS BOOK

Alexandra van Rennes (pages 160–169)
    @alexandravanrennes and @petithanout
Anneke Herbers (pages 114–123) @herberslifestyle.nl
Carla Rossiter (pages 138–147) @shedhomewares_e17
Catherine Ashton (pages 62–71) @bo__decor
Clare Lattin (pages 72–81) @Lattin72
Jo Moorfoot (pages 94–103) @settlenorfolk
Margo Hupert (pages 150–159) @margo.hupert.art
Marion Visser (pages 126–137) @stoerwonenenleven
Olga Turner (pages 104–113) @_ekkist
Sam Thompson (pages 82–91) @londonstylesisters

FURTHER INSPIRATION

@tintaluhrman
@wattleanddaubhome
@number5_cromwellhouse
@harpstudio
@the_idle_hands
@ingredientsldn
@myscandinavianhome
@labellevueneffies
@lobsterandswan
@violetdent

@marialemesurier
@thymka
@ninaanouk
@oumaimae_home
@edith__myhomestyle
@rossfarm_
@kinship_creativedc
@snickergladjen
@lumierelodge
@villa61.it

BUSINESS CREDITS

CATHERINE ASHTON
IG: @bo_decor
Page 3c, 18a, 23ar, 23br, 26a, 35b, 37br, 42, 43c, 46ar, 51b, 58, 60–71, 171.

DUCKSOUP
41 Dean Street
London W1D 4PY
T: +44 (0)20 7287 4599
Ducksoupsoho.co.uk
IG: @ducksoupsoho
and
Little Duck / The Picklery
68 Dalston Lane
London E8 3AH
T: +44 (0)20 7249 9177
Littleduckpicklery.co.uk
IG: @littleduckthepicklery
Pages 10, 12b, 15ar, 15br, 18c, 21br, 22, 24, 37ar, 39ar, 44bl, 52al, 53, 55al, 55cl, 72–81.

HERBERS LIFESTYLE
T: +31 (0)599 417137
E: info@herberslifestyle.nl
Herberslifestyle.nl
Pages 2, 3l, 29al, 30al, 30bl, 41, 46al, 46b, 47, 55ar, 55br, 114–123.

MARGO HUPERT
Margohupert.pl
IG: @margo.hupert.art
Endpapers, 1, 5, 6, 11b, 16, 19, 23bl, 28, 30br, 35c, 36, 44ar, 45, 48, 51c, 52b, 55cr, 57, 59, 148–149, 174.

PETIT HANOUT
Interior & Lifestyle Shop
De Melksuiker 36,
1911 ER Uitgeest
The Netherlands
T: +31 (0)6 30702129

E: info@petithanout.nl
Petithanout.nl
Pages 13, 14, 26c, 37al, 37bl, 160–169.

CARLA ROSSITER
IG: @shedhomewares_E17
Pages 4, 11a, 12a, 15al, 15 bl, 20, 21a, 21bl, 30ar, 30cl, 33, 39al, 138–147, 176.

SAM THOMPSON
IG: @LondonStyleSisters
Pages 18b, 38, 44al, 44br, 52ar, 82–91.

SETTLE
Larling Road
Shropham
Attleborough
Norfolk NR17 1EA
T: +44 (0)1953 497030

E: hello@settlenorfolk.co.uk
Settlenorfolk.co.uk
IG: settlenorfolk
Pages 3r, 7, 29ar, 29b, 50, 54, 55bl, 92–112.

**OLGA TURNER &
JONATHAN BAKER**
Ekkist Design Consultancy
10 Arthur Street
London EC4R 9AY
T: +44 (0)1483 560 249
E: ask@ekkist.co
Ekkist.co
IG: _ekkist
Pages 51a, 104–113.

MARION VISSER
IG: @stoerwonenenleven
Pages 8, 23al, 26b, 27, 30cr, 31, 34, 35a, 39b, 43a, 43b, 124–137.

INDEX

ACKNOWLEDGMENTS

We would like to begin with a huge thank you to the whole Ryland Peters & Small team for believing in our idea, supporting us on our shoots and making this book look and read its best.

Secondly, thank you to all the fantastic homeowners for inviting us to capture their beautiful houses. You were such amazing hosts and listening to your stories about what every home detail means to you was wonderful. It is this home-making history that truly inspires us. Appreciating the humble things as much as the highly prized is something instilled in us by our parents, to whom we are eternally indebted.

Thanks also go to all our followers and friends, for all their comments and support over the years. We hope our book inspires you and we would love to see your ideas and pictures. Find us on Instagram and Facebook @thecontentednest #homeforthesoul

Finally, we are so very grateful for the support of our own families and friends, keeping our homes and children cared for while we were away making this book. And it is to our children and their generation we would like to dedicate this book. We hope they will learn to appreciate hand me downs, be considerate when creating and care for everything we treasure.

With love,
Sara and Dan
The CONTENTed Nest